GUS GILKESON AND
NICK WORMALD

FUNDING BUSINESS GROWTH

*How to secure finance
to scale your business*

Rethink

First published in Great Britain in 2025
by Rethink Press (www.rethinkpress.com)

© Copyright Gus Gilkeson and Nick Wormald

All rights reserved. No part of this publication may be reproduced, stored in or introduced into a retrieval system, or transmitted, in any form, or by any means (electronic, mechanical, photocopying, recording or otherwise) without the prior written permission of the publisher.

The right of Gus Gilkeson and Nick Wormald to be identified as the authors of this work has been asserted by them in accordance with the Copyright, Designs and Patents Act 1988.

This book is sold subject to the condition that it shall not, by way of trade or otherwise, be lent, resold, hired out, or otherwise circulated without the publisher's prior consent in any form of binding or cover other than that in which it is published and without a similar condition including this condition being imposed on the subsequent purchaser.

Cover image © Shutterstock | Anton Starikov and Atstock

Contents

Introduction	1
PART ONE Understand	7
1 The Problem	9
Time	13
Freedom	20
Summary	22
2 Money: The Lifeblood Of A Business	25
Profit, cash flow and working capital cycles	27
Funding different business models	33
Profit is good, but cash is king	35
Summary	42

3	**The Value Of Money**	**43**
	Assets and liabilities	45
	Income and expenses	48
	Knowing when a business is ready to grow	52
	Summary	62
PART TWO	**Arrange**	**63**
4	**Preparation For Lending**	**65**
	Lending criteria	65
	5Cs Credit Model	72
	What is meant by 'lender ready'?	77
	Summary	79
5	**Sourcing Money For A Business**	**81**
	Cash/equity	81
	Grants and subsidies	83
	Strategic partnerships/joint ventures	84
	Innovation/diversification	85
	Marketing and sales	86
	Raising finance or capital	86
	Summary	95
6	**Debt Finance Products**	**97**
	Letters of credit (LC)	99
	Venture debt and private credit	103

	Seller or vendor financing	104
	Types of loan	107
	Other options: Trade finance and import–export finance	116
	Summary	119
7	**Specialised Funding, Ownership And IP**	**121**
	Fuelling growth in the building industry	124
	Invoice financing	126
	Considerations	129
	Summary	133

PART THREE Fund — **135**

8	**Who Will Lend Me Money?**	**137**
	Private lenders	138
	A bank of other potential lenders	140
	Who else will lend me money?	142
	Summary	145
9	**Ticking The Boxes**	**147**
	Supporting a loan	150
	Tax management for business growth and lending success	151
	Summary	156

10	**The Loan Process: Navigating The Final Stages**	**157**
	Loan document preparation	160
	Loan approval conditions: Understanding the requirements	164
	Maintain communication and follow up	167
	Summary	168

PART FOUR Grow — 171

11	**Growing Safely, And In The Right Order**	**173**
	The 5 Stages of Growth Model	174
	Key principles for growth planning	190
	Key considerations for defining growth objectives	191
	Driving successful business growth	193
	Summary	194

12	**Putting Money To Work**	**197**
	Be aware of opportunities	199
	90-day strategic review	202
	It's now game on	204
	Summary	207

13 Personal Growth — 209

- Vision — 210
- Drivers — 212
- Values — 213
- Goals — 214
- Blocks — 214
- Habits — 215
- Verticals — 216
- Congruency — 217
- Fit vs healthy vs well-being — 218
- Self-mastery — 219
- Finally… — 222
- Summary — 224

14 Goal-Setting 101 — 225

- Define your goals — 226
- Summary — 238

Conclusion — 239

Acknowledgements — 245

The Authors — 251

Introduction

As experienced and successful specialists in the finance broker industry, over the past decade we have enabled numerous business owners and investors to grow their companies through funding. This is why so many of our clients have been with us for the long term. But we don't just help others. We are also business owners ourselves, and, as such, we walk the talk, applying the same principles to our own business that we share with clients.

We have known each other since our teens. In our early working lives, we embraced finance and corporate technology, respectively, before Gus founded Grow Capital with a mission to help business owners harness capital growth opportunities via funding. We guarantee results because we are invested in our clients.

Now we want to enable you to achieve success. To do this, you need to understand where and how to grow without compromising either yourself or your company. This is where we can help.

Funding Business Growth arms you with the tools and resources required to take your business to the next level and beyond, using tested and proven financing options. Divided into four parts – Understand, Arrange, Fund, Grow – we walk through a range of real-world success stories from business owners showcasing how they have used the tools in this book to unlock massive growth, gain back some much-needed time, and finally grasp that one elusive goal: financial freedom.

We provide you with a framework to achieve success in three primary pain points that are faced by over 90% of businesses: time, money and freedom. Exploring available funding options and how to identify when a business is ready to grow, as well as the importance of

BUSINESS STAGNATION

- **Strong Cash Flow**
- **Financial Freedom**
- **Unlock Time**

FUND

- Dedicated Team
- Admin Team
- Professional
- Streamline Process

Analyse / Report / Tender / Manage

UNDERSTAND

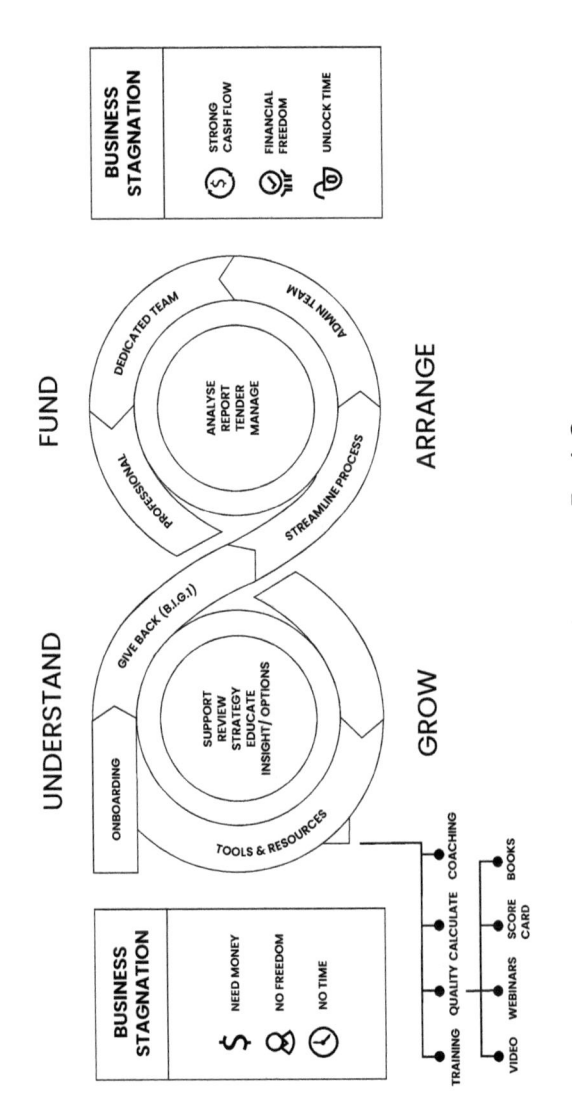

- Give Back (B.I.G.I)
- Onboarding

ARRANGE

GROW

Support / Review / Strategy / Educate / Insight / Options

Tools & Resources:
- Training — Video
- Quality Calculate — Webinars
- Coaching — Score Card
- Books

BUSINESS STAGNATION

- **Need Money**
- **No Freedom**
- **No Time**

Understand, Arrange, Fund, Grow

growing in the right order, are key components of this book. We also delve into our 5Cs Credit Model, which determines the credibility of loan applicants. Through each chapter, we provide you with a detailed guide that will instil confidence when implementing strategies and accessing capital.

In essence, *Funding Business Growth* is a how-to manual, educating readers step by step on the basics of business finance and growth. By reading this book and following our advice, you will acquire a blueprint that can be applied to, or overlaid across, any business. As a result, you will benefit from multiple returns on both your time and monetary investment. The value of this is more than just numbers on a spreadsheet; it means being in control of your business and its direction.

And there's more. We believe that the power of the mindset is crucial. This is why our holistic approach will ensure a more balanced and healthier attitude, focusing on looking after yourself, physically and mentally, as well as teach you to reverse engineer traditional business approaches to improve your lifestyle and relationships.

INTRODUCTION

We are excited to partner with you, imparting our experience and knowledge to help you to grow your business safely. No matter your industry, or how busy you are, whether you are a business owner or investor, if you are focused on growing, then we can help you achieve your aims.

This is our legacy. We live and breathe our principles. We want you to do the same.

PART ONE
UNDERSTAND

'How do I grow my business?' This is the question that we hear most often in our work with small business owners – and it's one that isn't as simple as you might think. So, to begin with, let's understand what it means to grow your business and how you can go about doing it.

1
The Problem

Business growth can be measured in several ways. The first question you need to ask yourself is, *How do I define the growth of my business?*

- More sales?
- More staff?
- More profit?
- More revenue?
- More 'likes'/social presence?
- More media coverage?

The second question is, *What do I really want from this growth?*

- More time to spend with family, friends?
- More money to spend or give?
- More freedom to do what you want?

People generally go into business so they can live the life of their dreams, working from a laptop on some beautiful beach two days a week, watching the money mountains pile up and being able to do whatever they want, whenever they want.

It all sounds so easy when you first listen to the 'gurus' of business – do this, add that and, *bam!* You're done! It often doesn't take long for a fledgling business owner to realise that business can be harder than it looks, and if you don't get it right, the dream can soon become a nightmare.

There are, however, a few people out there that reach this magical place of business success. These are the ones you see on social media, on the news with their amazing 'gutter-to-glitter' story earning them fame and untold wealth.

THE PROBLEM

After working with thousands of businesses over the last twenty or more years, I've noticed certain patterns starting to emerge with businesses large and small, from all different sectors, and in particular the ones that were attempting to grow.

All these businesses found themselves having similar problems, a myriad of issues in and around their day-to-day operations, and it became apparent to me that all these issues stemmed in some form from one of these three issues:

1. Shortage of time
2. Absence of freedom
3. Lack of money

We'll look at each of these in turn, starting with the first two – time and freedom – in this chapter, and we'll look at money in Chapter 2. For now, here are some examples of these issues from the real world:

'My customers want to triple their monthly order going forward. How am I supposed to cover the payment

> to suppliers when my invoices are not paid for sixty days?'
>
> 'I need to hire five sales staff to get our new product line out to market before our competitor beats us to it. Where am I going to find the time to recruit these people?'
>
> 'I haven't had a day off with my family in two years – if I take time off, the business just grinds to a halt.'
>
> 'I don't have a decent salesperson in my team – as a business owner, it's all up to me.'
>
> 'Right now, I have no idea where my business is at financially.'
>
> 'Training my team is frustrating; it takes forever and often the results are not great.'

Sound familiar? If you answered yes, you're not alone! We hear statements like the above most days, in some format, from most businesses we deal with out there – large and small.

Why do we need to solve these problems?

For a business to be successful, it must have proven systems and processes that don't rely on one person, and these need to be repeatable and scalable. Why? Because of the one thing that is available to all of us. Read on.

Time

Time is the one common denominator that keeps us all on the same playing field. Every single person on the Earth has a maximum of twenty-four hours in a day. No more, no less. Whether you are a billionaire or a small child in a Mumbai slum, those twenty-four hours are all you have with which to do all that you want and need to do.

Some people like to fill every moment with busy work, jamming life full of their stuff, while others like to leave big holes in their day to fill with stillness and quiet.

Many will argue the most valuable resource in the world is time. You can get more money, you can hire more team members, but you cannot buy more hours in a day. If you're a business owner wanting to grow your business, and the business relies upon you in one or more areas to expand, you are going to run out of time at some point. It may not be now. It may not be next month. But it will happen eventually.

> **TOP TIP**
>
> The aim of the game as a business owner is to work in the *right* areas of your business at the *right* time. Test the value and effectiveness of each area of your business, measure your processes, inputs and outputs in the different areas, record your results against targets and test whether you can replicate your success, and then replace yourself in that area.

If you can do that once successfully, you can do it often. And your business can scale.

Everyone is different, yet what is certain is that, as a business owner, you have a finite number of hours to get stuck in and hustle. Managing your time is vital, so ask yourself:

- How many hours a day do you spend working *in* vs *on* your business?

- What percentage of your working day is kept open/free?

- How would your business fare if you had more time?

THE PROBLEM

We often ask business owners where they spend most of their time and why. Their response? *'Everywhere!'*

A famous quote often misattributed to the late, great author and thinker on management, Peter Drucker, is, 'What gets measured gets managed', and while it seems he never actually said this, it is a simple truism that serves as an important starting point for nearly every business we talk to.

Ask yourself this:

- How do you measure your time, and the time your team puts into your business?
- When was the last time you physically tracked the time taken on individual tasks in your business?

We have found this absence of time measuring in most businesses (including our own).

One of Peter Drucker's best-known students in business circles was American business leader, author and coach, Stephen Covey. Stephen was the hugely successful owner of a company named Franklin Covey, and he authored more than fifteen books on business management and strategy.

In his best-selling book *The 7 Habits of Highly Effective People*, Covey introduces us to the Time Management Quadrants.[1]

The basic premise of the quadrants is that time and tasks can be divided into four quadrants as follows:

- **Quadrant 1:** Important and urgent
- **Quadrant 2:** Important and not urgent
- **Quadrant 3:** Not important and urgent
- **Quadrant 4:** Not important and not urgent

To be an effective leader, you should be spending most of your time in Quadrant 2 doing **important** tasks that are **non-urgent**.

What tasks are in that quadrant? Here are a few examples:

- Planning

---

[1] S Covey, *The 7 Habits of Highly Effective People*, 15th edition (Free Press, 2004)

THE PROBLEM

- Educating (yourself and others) through training and professional development
- Building relationships
- Building business assets

Ask yourself this: How often do you dedicate time for each of the above? Here's the most common response we hear to this question: 'I would do all these if I could just find the time, but I'm too busy running my business.'

So, the million-dollar question is – how do we free up time to do these priority tasks?

Measure, record, outsource

The way to free up time is by following the steps we, the authors, take:

1. We measure exactly what we are doing that day and during a normal business cycle in our company (more on business cycles later).
2. We measure how long it takes us to do each of those tasks. This is called a 'Time and Motion Study'.

3. We look for patterns and identify the repetitive tasks. These are often the 'boring' tasks in business.

4. We record how to do these tasks – from start to finish – in the best and most efficient way possible.

5. We outsource these tasks to someone else, such as the right team member or an external consultant who manages those tasks going forward.

6. *Boom!* Once we have handed those tasks to someone else, we have the time back that we used to spend doing them, and we can focus on the important stuff!

So, why doesn't everyone do this?

A common objection we hear from business owners is: 'What I do is very specialised, there's no way someone else could do what I do.'

Agreed! In fact, we freely admit we used to think this way ourselves. Corporate finance and business advisory are famous for this view – ask any highly paid management consultant!

We have found that:

- The more you start getting your thoughts and processes down and recorded (could be by video, a paper training manual, voice recording, online platform, flowchart, or a combination of things), the more you realise how repetitious these tasks are.

- While you might do a task in your business slightly differently to someone else, such as a competitor or other team member, there is often a baseline, a process that can generally be followed by someone else if explained in the right way.

As a business owner, if you can record and get even some of the daily, repeatable, low-value processes off your plate, you free up your time to focus on the important parts of your business.

Freedom

What is freedom?

Freedom is having the ability to act or change without constraint. If someone or something is 'free', it can change easily and is not constrained in its present state. A person has the freedom to do things that will not, in theory or in practice, be prevented by other forces.

Think back to when you first had the idea that you wanted to start a business. What were your primary drivers? Were you looking to escape the corporate world or launch a new idea, or maybe you were just interested in doing what you do better than anyone else?

One of the most common reasons we hear is 'to obtain freedom':

- Freedom to make decisions
- Freedom to do what you want
- Financial freedom

Most new businesses are started by an individual with a dream of freedom, but after three to five years, this dream has faded from mind leaving a swirling pool of thoughts, bills, worries and business stuff. Freedom is also something that most do not think about regularly, an elusive gem that needs to be identified before it's uncovered and brought into the daylight.

We have identified a list of common reasons people lack the freedom they once dreamed of:

- They are stuck in the workplace, doing many more hours than they want.
- They are unable to think freely and clearly due to an ever-growing list of problems.
- They are always on the phone talking to clients, suppliers and staff.
- They are always dealing with interruptions from untrained staff and clients.
- They have long, unnecessary meetings taking up precious time.
- They procrastinate.

TOP TIP

Many reasons for the absence of freedom can be easily solved with planning, courage and the right tools.

If you had an extra two hours in the day, what would be the top three things you could do that would move the needle for you and improve the growth of your business? For instance:

- Travelling at different times
- Playing more sport or going to the gym
- Spending more time with family
- Spending some time with a coach or mentor to make a longer-term plan for your business

A lot of business owners don't spend much time planning where they want to go and what they would like to do.

Part of the process of winning back your freedom is looking at your daily business activities and aligning these with your short-term and long-term goals (including your business exit strategy), which we will delve into later.

Summary

- Define your business growth then decide what you want from that growth.

THE PROBLEM

- You have no more or less time than anybody else. How you use your time is the key.
- Free your time via measuring, recording and outsourcing.
- With the right planning, you can regain your freedom.

2
Money: The Lifeblood Of A Business

Let's turn our attention now to the last of the three issues we identified in the last chapter: money.

Money is a medium that can be exchanged for goods and services and be used as a measure of their value on the market.

How important is this medium to a business?

- If the flow of money into a business *slows*, it will struggle.

- If the flow of money into a business is *irregular*, it will suffocate.

- If the flow of money into a business *stops*, it will die.

Money is the lifeblood of any business, and having enough of it is vital, as is having a consistent, steady flow of it to ensure all commitments are met. When a business cannot meet its financial commitments, it is deemed to be insolvent, which indicates that a business is likely finished. For some businesses, this financial distress is apparent and frequent, while for others it can be hidden from view until it's too late.

To avoid this, we aim for:

- A *sufficient* supply of money in the business to keep up with commitments
- The ability to *measure the supply* of money regularly to keep a business healthy

Let's look at how this works in reality... How does a business receive money? Here are a few common ways:

- Sales of products/services
- Investors contributing money

- Government grants and subsidies
- Loans
- Owners investing money

According to the Reserve Bank of Australia (RBA), most small businesses lack the money required to grow, but this doesn't have to be the case.

Profit, cash flow and working capital cycles

Understanding a business involves understanding its 'profitability', its 'cash flow' and its 'working capital cycle'.

Profit

Profit is the amount of money the business makes after paying its expenses. The primary reason most businesses are in existence is to make a profit, and to use that profit to build assets, and to build the shareholders' net wealth. If you don't believe us, simply ask any business owner if they would continue to do what they do day-to-day if the business wasn't getting paid.

Most of them would say, '*No way!* I would prefer to sit on the beach!' (Sadly, many business owners aren't making money and are working for free, unknowingly.)

If we look at what profit is specifically, it's basically the income of a business less the expenses. The profit earned can be used for several things, such as buying new company assets, paying down existing liabilities, paying dividends or bonuses to shareholders, owners, employees, etc, or a combination of any of those things.

Cash flow

Cash flow is when the business receives its money. But how do we measure cash flow specifically in a business?

When someone commits to buy from your business, they either buy on cash terms or payment terms (over time). That commitment to buy forms what is called an 'account receivable' for your business – you are waiting to receive the account payment. Could be a minute, could be months.

Now you have a commitment to purchase, you've got to pay to produce or deliver that product or service. This is what we call an 'account payable'... your business needs to pay your suppliers to produce the goods or services you have promised.

Your accounts receivable less your accounts payable is your effective 'point in time' cash position.

Working capital

The working capital cycle is how long it takes, from start to finish, for a business to provide their good or service, pay their expenses and get paid. The timing of payments and receivables can vary wildly and the measurement of that specifically is what we call cash flow timing, a cash conversion, or a working capital cycle.

As a basic example, a working capital cycle looks at your suppliers and how your agreement operates with those suppliers, service providers or manufacturers, how you distribute your goods or service and who your end customer is. It also looks at how your arrangement works with your customers and consumers, how they pay you (up front or when they receive the goods?), and what the profit margin on your products is.

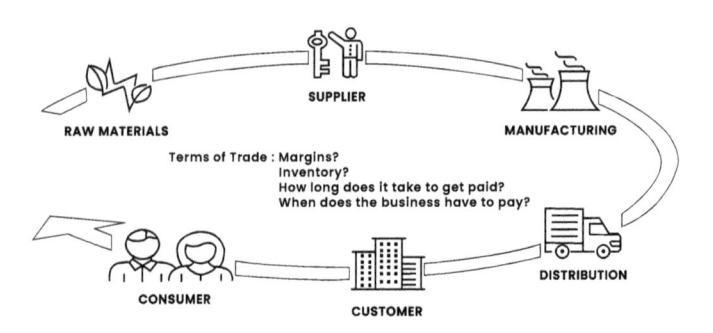

Working capital cycle

So, let's look at a couple of examples of the flow of products through the supply chain and how they can look similar but can be different.

In the first example, we've got a traditional supply chain in which someone buys or manufactures stock and then sells it based on anticipated future demand.

The second scenario is more popular these days – the 'just-in-time' or 'demand-driven' supply chain. You know the sort – they're the likes of your more digitalised platforms

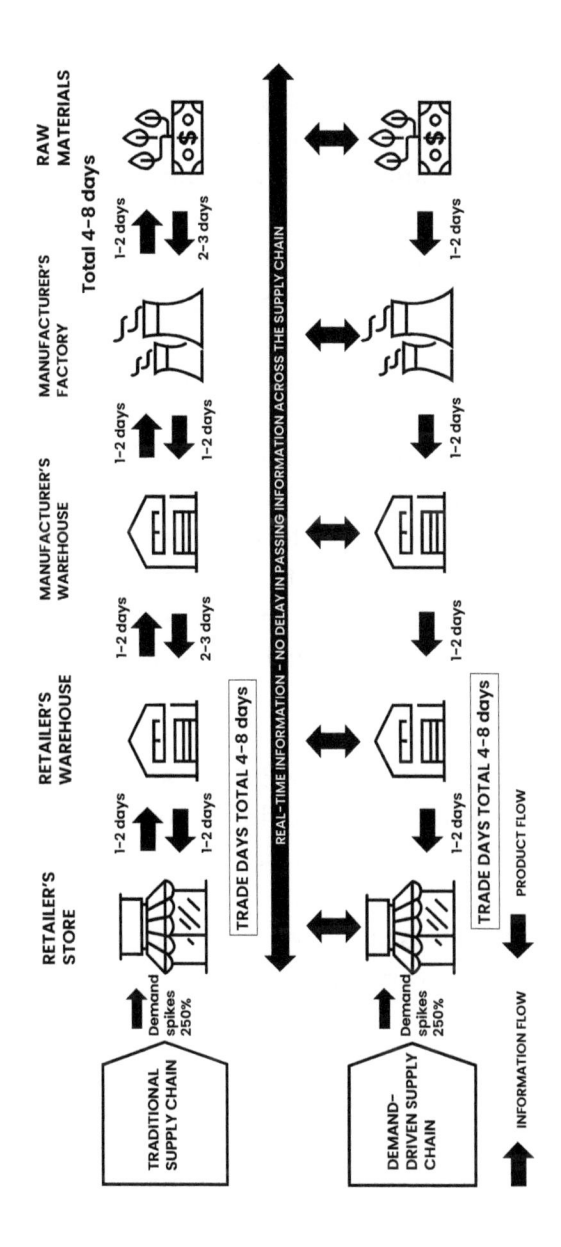

Flow of payments (cash conversion cycle) in a supply chain – traditional supply chain vs just-in-time (demand-driven) supply chain

whereby someone places an order, and once that order is placed, the product is manufactured in real-time and there's no delay in passing information through the supply chain.

So, as you can see, in a traditional supply chain, if there's a demand spike, it takes one to two days to communicate this to the retailer's warehouse, and then they have to go to the manufacturer and say, 'Hey, we need more stock!' And then the manufacturers have to purchase the raw materials. When the raw materials are delivered to the manufacturer and improved/made into something, only then can they be sent to the retailer's warehouse, and finally they can be delivered to the retail store.

That trade or supply chain turnaround in that traditional model could be somewhere between ten and eighteen days.

In the newer demand-driven supply chain, the process can be very different.

If all the processes are *recorded*, *enabled*, and *integrated* properly, the minute the order is placed, then the raw material is produced. The factory probably knows what its stock levels are and is more prepared, and the raw materials are shipped to the manufacturer faster than to the retailer's warehouse, within a couple of days.

In this example, the extra efficiency means that you're cutting down the time it takes to deliver your product to the end client by anywhere from six to fourteen days – so, about half.

> **TOP TIP**
>
> By speeding up the information flow in your supply chain, with all the parties, the product flow is faster.

Funding different business models

Some of the key questions that you're going to get asked in relation to funding are:

- What are your terms of trade?
- What is the average margin on your product?
- How long does it normally take you to get paid for that product?

- How much inventory do you hold? Is that your own inventory or is that on behalf of your client?

- When does the business have to pay for an order once it's been put in? Is it now? Is it down the track when the manufactured goods are received?

- Where are your wholesale goods or contracted services coming from and what is the timeline on that?

Traditional supply chains usually mean a high-margin business. It might be a low-volume business, but it has a higher margin of 50%. In this case, they take a while to get paid. The demand-driven supply chain, on the other hand, is a high-volume, low-margin sales 10% margin, but they get paid upfront, immediately upon ordering, and they pay on delivery of the goods then pay the supplier.

We'll just walk through a couple of examples and how most businesses measure these metrics.

The primary way businesses report business cash flow and cash flow timing is in a

Business Cash Flow Statement (historical results) and a Business Cash Flow Forecast (expected future results). These reports show cash positioning with money going out and coming in along with the timings, whether that's monthly, weekly, daily, or whatever it is, depending on what the report looks like.

Now, every business needs to make a profit, but profit isn't everything as we will discuss in the next section.

Profit is good, but cash is king

You can have the most profitable business in the world but if it takes you ten years to get paid, you are going to starve to death and go out of business before you receive any profit! This extreme example of a payment delay demonstrates what we call a cash flow gap.

> **TOP TIP**
> The more efficient the cash flow cycle, the fewer gaps, the easier it is in terms of payment options, and the faster you get paid.

How do we measure these gaps, and therefore the efficiency in your business or in your supply chain?

Well, one of the key ways we do this is using a cash-conversion cycle calculation. This is basically a measurement of the amount of time it takes a company to convert their inventory and assets to cash.

We use a couple of common metrics to calculate that, and the formula is as follows:

> Days of Inventory Outstanding (DIO) +
> Days of Sales Outstanding (DSO) −
> Days Payable Outstanding (DPO)
> = Cash Conversion Cycle (CCC)

From this calculation we get an answer measured in days. The lower the number of days, the more efficient the business, because that's the number of days it takes to complete a full cash flow cycle.

So, for example, where:

- DIO = 45 days (average inventory holding time)

- DSO = 30 days (average time for customers to pay)
- DPO = 40 days (average time to pay suppliers)

The calculation would be:

45 days + 30 days − 40 days = 35 days

Now let's have another look at the two examples in the earlier 'flow of payments' figure. In the traditional supply chain, we might have thought this is a higher margin business; they've said they're making a 50% margin. However, if we look at that calculation of efficiency, it tells a bit of a different story.

Looking at the example business in the figure, which has a 50% margin, they're holding about three months' worth of stock in their warehouse at any given time – this is their Days Inventory Outstanding. We've called it fifty-four days, which is the total supply chain of eighteen days, times three (around three months).

In this case, Days of Sales Outstanding shows that it takes the average client about fifty days to pay after they place an order, and then the business needs to pay their suppliers/manufacturers within thirty days.

So that cash-conversion cycle calculation is a total of seventy-four days. Now, if you look at how that looks in terms of efficiency, per annum, per $100k of orders, they make $50,000 on every $100,000 of orders. And they make that every seventy-four days.

So, what does that equate to over 365 days of the year? That's effectively $246,622 on total turnover of $493,000. So yes, high margin. But in this case, because time is a limiting factor, the turnover is only $493,000 – it's taking them longer to produce their products, and it's taking them longer to get paid.

Now let's look at the same company using a demand-driven supply chain, or the just-in-time supply chain. Here, they've got a shorter trade cycle, their margin is smaller, but they're doing a higher volume of sales.

In this case, they don't hold any stock. When an order comes in, it goes straight through to the manufacturer who then builds that product and sends it out to the warehouse, who

MONEY: THE LIFEBLOOD OF A BUSINESS

then sends it to retail. Once that's done, they get their payment.

At the very latest, most of the time, these types of businesses get paid a decent portion of the overall product price upfront, if not the whole lot.

But in this case, let's assume a worst-case scenario – that they get paid eight days after an order is placed, when they have delivered the item. And in terms of Days Payable Outstanding, well, they've got to pay the suppliers for this stuff pretty much straightaway as well. So, we'll say that needs paying on day one as well, as soon as the order comes in.

Now we've got Days Inventory Outstanding of one, plus Days Sales Outstanding of eight – that's nine minus the one day they have to pay the suppliers. *That's eight days in total.*

In terms of efficiency, for every $100,000, they're only making $10,000... However, in this case, they are making that *every eight days*, which is $456,250, which is a total turnover of $4.56 million over the course of a 365-day year.

FUNDING BUSINESS GROWTH

A 10% margin sounds like they're making a lot less, but because of the efficiency in their supply chain, their cash-conversion cycle is a lot faster in this specific example.

So that's just a couple of examples of how money and time can have a dramatic impact on any business.

Some of the key questions you might get asked, or you probably need to know in your business for supply chain include:

- How would you describe your business?
- Is it high margin, low volume?
- Or is it low margin with a higher volume? Or is it a combination of both?
- What are the barriers to creating the volume you need in your business?
- Do you need to scale that up? Do you need to scale it up rapidly? What is the margin on your sales, roughly?
- How much inventory are you holding on average?
- How many days does it take you to turn over your stock, on average?

MONEY: THE LIFEBLOOD OF A BUSINESS

- When a client purchases from you, how long does it take them to receive goods or services?

- How long does it take you to receive payment from them in full?

- Conversely, when someone orders from you and you need the materials from your suppliers/manufacturers, how soon do you have to pay for that item or those items?

- Do you have standard terms of contracts across all your clients?

- Do you have standard terms and conditions of trade with your suppliers?

Once you understand your profitability, cash flow and working capital cycle, what options does your business have to solve its money problems?

- Sales of products/services – sell more of what you offer, faster and more efficiently.

- Investors – have people invest money in your business.

- Government grants and subsidies – seek support from industry and government.

- Loans – borrow to grow the business and build assets.
- Owners' contribution – the owners put in some of their own money.

We'll talk about each of these in detail later.

Summary

- Ensure you have a sufficient supply of money flowing into your business.
- Efficiency in production will have a positive impact on your working capital cycle.
- Understanding profitability, business cash flow and the working capital cycle in your business can make all the difference.
- Cash is king, regardless of profit.

3
The Value Of Money

As we have established, money is the lifeblood of a business. Without a free flow of cash sufficient to cover all expenses and liabilities, a business becomes insolvent and is likely to die. Money is also a trading tool used to buy stock, supplies, assets and even to invest.

Now let's focus on how integral money is to the operation of a business, how it can be used to fuel growth and expansion, expand into new markets and a myriad of other uses.

So, why does a business need money, and why is it so important?

> **TOP TIP**
>
> A business can grow more easily with the right framework in place.

Picture this, it's a Monday morning, you have your cup of coffee steaming away in front of you and you are standing in front of your whiteboard, staring at the two words you have written: *Business growth*

Achieving this is your absolute number-one goal. After six months of negotiating with your clients, you have a massive opportunity sitting right in front of you and are committed to making it a reality. You have updated your business plan, written a new marketing and sales strategy, set up cash flow forecasting for the next twenty-four months, identified the first key hire and spoken to your suppliers about your strategy.

All these changes in your business will cost money, however, of which you have little left at the end of each month. You need an injection of funds and, unfortunately, all the original sources of capital (your own money and that of your family and friends etc) are now tapped out.

The time has come to look at external sources of finance.

In front of you are three burning questions:

1. Is my business ready to grow?
2. What financing options are available to me?
3. How do I get money into the business?

We're going to look at the first of these in this chapter, and we'll explore the others in Part 2: Arrange. But before we get started on that, there are a few important words you are likely to hear and need to know when funding a growing business.

Assets and liabilities

Assets

An asset is a valuable resource that is owned and is under the control of a business. This resource has an economic value and benefits the business.

FUNDING BUSINESS GROWTH

Assets are reported on a company's balance sheet, identifying both the asset's current value and any liability associated with it. Ideally, an asset can generate income for the business without the need for input by staff or owners.

There are a few types of assets:

- Current assets:
  - Cash and cash equivalents
  - Receivables
  - Inventory
  - Pre-paid expense

- Fixed assets:
  - Plant and equipment
  - Vehicles
  - Property

- Financial assets:
  - Stocks
  - Bonds
  - Hybrid securities

- Intangible assets:
  - Patents
  - Trademarks
  - Copyrights

- Goodwill
- IP

Liabilities

Liabilities can be categorised into different types based on their expiration or due date. Current liabilities refer to short-term debts and obligations that are due within one year, or the normal operating cycle of a business. Examples of current liabilities include accounts payable, short-term loans, payments on long-term debt, accrued liabilities, income taxes, deferred revenue and commercial paper.

On the other hand, noncurrent liabilities, also known as long-term liabilities, are debts and obligations that are not due within the next year. They include obligations such as bonds, deferred tax, long-term debt, mortgages, leases, pensions, and other long-term financial commitments.

Additionally, there are contingent liabilities, which are special types of debts or obligations that may or may not occur in the future. These liabilities depend on certain events or circumstances. Examples of contingent liabilities include legal costs related to lawsuits and warranties for products.

Not all contingent liabilities need to be reported on a company's balance sheet. Generally accepted accounting principles (GAAP) require reporting only of probable contingent liabilities, which are events that are likely to happen and the costs of which can be reasonably estimated.

Possible and remote contingent liabilities are not required to be stated on the balance sheet but should be disclosed in the footnotes of financial statements.

Assets and liabilities must legally be recorded and reported by businesses on their financial statements, on what is called the 'balance sheet'.

Income and expenses

Income

Business income refers to the money earned by a business entity through its operations. It is a type of earned income and is classified as ordinary income for tax purposes.

Business income includes any income realised as a result of the entity's activities, such as revenue from the sale of products or services, fees received from professional practice, and rents received from real estate business.

Business income is calculated by subtracting the costs of doing business from the revenue generated. These costs may include expenses related to production, operation, marketing and administration. Business expenses and losses can offset business income, which can be either positive or negative in any given year.

The taxation of business income depends on the type of business entity.

Expenses

Expenses refer to the costs incurred by a business entity as a result of its operations. These expenses are necessary and ordinary costs that a company must bear to generate revenue and maintain its day-to-day activities.

> **TOP TIP**
>
> Business expenses can be deducted from the business's income to reduce its taxable income, thereby lowering the overall tax liability.

There are several types of business expenses:

- **General expenses:** These are costs associated with managing and supervising an operating business, including employee wages, salaries, super contributions and other expenditure related to employing staff.

- **Operating expenses (OPEX):** These expenses are essential for running the business and include items such as rent, utilities, marketing expenses, maintenance costs and vehicle expenses.

- **Capital expenses (CAPEX):** Capital expenses refer to the costs incurred when purchasing assets for the growth or profitability of the business. These types of purchases include equipment, machinery, furniture, vehicles, intellectual property, patents, manuals and real estate.

- **Inventory expenses:** These are the direct and indirect expenses associated with building and maintaining inventory (or trading stock) in the business, including storage costs, taxes and insurance policies.

While business inventory itself is not a tax-deductible expense, its value can be used to offset gross receipts. When claiming tax deductions for business expenses, there are some important considerations. The expenses must be directly related to earning income for the business, and proper records must be kept to substantiate the claims. If an expense has both business and private use, only the portion used for business purposes can be claimed.

Certain business expenses are not deductible, such as entertainment expenses (unless provided as a 'fringe benefit' and taxed separately), traffic fines, private or domestic expenses, and payments for which Pay As You Go (PAYG) Tax withholding or reporting obligations have not been met.

Expenses relating to capital assets that fall under capital gains tax rules may also have different treatment.

> **TOP TIP**
> Consult with a tax professional or the relevant tax authorities in your country or region for accurate and up-to-date information regarding business expense deductions.

The specific rules and regulations regarding deductible business expenses may vary by location. Income and expenses are legally recorded and reported by businesses on their financial statements on what is called the 'Profit and Loss Statement'.

Knowing when a business is ready to grow

Let's now return to the first of the burning questions we asked earlier, as we stood in front of our whiteboard: is my business ready to grow?

Opportunities always make themselves known when you least expect it. Being prepared to take advantage of an opportunity is the hallmark of a true entrepreneur.

Financial indicators for being growth-ready come in a variety of forms, however some of the general basic financial indicators in a business are:

- The business is earning more than it spends, income is stable or growing, and expenditure is stable or growing at a slower rate than income.

- The business's assets are greater than its liabilities.

- The business gets paid as soon as possible after a sale.

- The business's suppliers offer great terms.

Business cash flow and their timings are recorded and reported by businesses on their financial statements, on what is called the 'cash flow statement'.

Five stages of business growth

Like people, businesses go through stages of growth and maturity. Different stages have different characteristics and, more importantly, different needs if they are to grow.

The five stages can best be identified and summarised as:

1. Existence (start-ups)
2. Survival (viability)
3. Success (stabilise or grow)
4. Scale (expansion)
5. Maturity

Let's have a look at some key elements of these now, as well as some common questions and tips relating to each.

Stage 1: Existence (start-ups)

- Characterised by feelings of fear and self-doubt.
- The organisation is simple, with generally fewer than five people.
- The concept and product/process are often unproven.
- There are no formal processes, systems or planning.

THE VALUE OF MONEY

- The strategy is to find money to survive.
- The owner *is* the business, doing everything.
- Huge time commitments.

Common questions at this stage include:

- What is the right product?
- How do we find the right customers?
- How can we finance operations until we have revenue?
- Will we survive?

Tips:

- Stay active and generate awareness in your target market.
- Test, validate and adjust the product or service.
- Act when opportunities appear.
- Ask questions – lots of them!
- Stay positive, curious and flexible.

Stage 2: Survival (viability)

- Characterised by feelings of optimism and excitement.
- The organisation is still simple.
- There are minimal systems and processes in place.
- The strategy is to find more leads.
- The owner makes all the decisions.

Common questions at this stage include:

- Can we generate enough cash flow to stay in business long term?
- How do we find and qualify more leads?
- What marketing strategy do I aim for?
- How do I start hiring staff?

Tips:

- Differentiate yourself from your competitors. Develop a unique selling proposition.
- Ensure expenses are reviewed often and kept under tight control.

- Use software to manage and forecast cash flow.
- Consider cash flow and/or receivables funding to stabilise/smooth out cash flow as required.

Companies at the survival stage either grow past this stage into stage 3, or they stay in survival, where the owner gives up and the company is either sold or dissolved.

Stage 3: Success (stabilise or grow)

- Characterised by a feeling that there is no time to enjoy cash flow.
- The organisation is now making money.
- Sales and marketing processes are bedded down, although often not documented.
- The strategy is to hire the right people.
- The owner is like a hamster on a wheel, constantly working to keep things moving.

Common questions at this stage include:

- Do we capitalise on our current success and grow, or stay stable and profitable?

- How do I reduce the hours that I am working while keeping the business afloat?
- What parts of the business do I systemise first?
- How do I find and keep good people?
- What financial resources do I need to grow?
- What areas do I grow first?

Tips:

- Focus on your systems, systems, systems!
- Make a key hire of an operations manager to start taking on some of your load.
- Look at multiple financial options – equity, debt, cash flow.

Stage 4: Scale (expansion)

- Characterised by a feeling of being out of control.
- The organisation is now making money and the drivers of the revenue and costs are clearly identified.

- Sales and marketing processes are bedded down and documented.
- The strategy is to hire more of the right people in more locations.
- The owner has or is looking for a management team to 'steer the ship'.

Common questions at this stage include:

- What growth channels will we use – in-person, online, new products?
- Are our existing systems adequate?
- What parts of the business still need to be systemised?
- How do I find and keep good people?
- Is outsourcing part of our process(es) a better option?

Tips:

- Have your systems and processes clearly mapped and weak areas identified.
- Consider external specialists/consultants to develop better processes/products.

- Look into corporate financing solutions for the areas required.

Stage 5: Maturity

- A common feeling is doubt about how big you are growing and whether you are horizontally or vertically integrating.
- Established corporate governance and business intelligence dashboards drive business.
- Processes are documented with redundancies and there are flexible channel and partner strategies.
- The strategy is to establish effective corporate governance, leaders and teams.
- The owner moves to a chairperson-style role – day-to-day operations and management are run by 'C level' executives.

Common questions at this stage include:

- Where will we find growth to meet revenue targets and shareholder return expectations?

- Are our systems and governance controls in place?
- How do we manage our reputation and reputational risk?
- Are our people and our culture right?
- Are our partners aligned?

Tips:

- Have a strong board, steering committees and working committees.
- Review external systems, specialists/consultants, processes/products.
- Look into corporate and investment banking financing solutions for the areas required.

As you can see, each of these five stages of business growth is different. Progress through the stages might be fast, slow or varied, depending on your industry and other factors specific to your business.

Strategic financing and planning are also varied and different for each stage, however a lot of the principles remain similar.

Summary

- Always have a sufficient flow of cash to cover your outgoings and liabilities.

- Being a successful entrepreneur means staying alert for opportunities.

- Understand where your business is at in order to ascertain the possibilities of growth.

PART TWO
ARRANGE

An injection of money can fuel business growth. To give you a head start, we'll share the 5Cs Credit Model and then explore the different sources of finance, from loans and credit to grants and subsidies.

4
Preparation For Lending

We're now going to return to the second of the burning questions from the last chapter: what financing options are available to me? We'll explore the criteria for lending, and how a borrower can figure out if they meet the criteria or not *before* going through the lengthy process of an application.

Lending criteria

The lending criteria, or qualifying criteria, are the items that any lender will use to assess an application for a loan. Lenders generally have unique lending criteria matched to their appetite for risk, regulatory conditions, their business needs, and various other internal requirements. For an outsider, these criteria can be a source of confusion, so we have developed a model to help simplify the requirements into five categories. This is known as the 5Cs Credit Model, and we will explain it in more detail shortly.

Meanwhile, the preparation for lending, and figuring out if you will meet the criteria is simplified by the following questions:

- How clear are you on what you are trying to achieve?
  - *What* are you buying?
  - *Why* are you buying it?
  - *When* will you buy it?
  - *How* will you pay it off?

- How do I find the right lender or lenders?
  - Research the lending market/google.
  - Connect with a finance broker.

You then need to obtain the lending criteria from the potential lenders you have identified, and match these off against your current situation, requirements and objectives.

PREPARATION FOR LENDING

For example, let's say that XYZ Corp is looking to buy the warehouse that they are currently leasing. XYZ Corp has been trading profitably for seven years, is up to date with their commitments and has a strong balance sheet. However, they have not yet finalised their financial statements and won't be able to for some time.

XYZ Corp's owners, John and Mary, think they need to borrow around $500,000, but they don't want to offer their home or any other property as security. John obtains the lending criteria from his broker and matches this off with his own requirements to see if it will work. John and Mary then compare the prospective lenders.

While Lender B is quite expensive, they are the only available lender that doesn't require real estate security, and they might therefore be more attractive to John and Mary. However, John and Mary may not be able to provide the financials and tax returns the lenders require for approval.

If John and Mary were willing to reconsider offering a property asset as security, they would be significantly better off with Lender D.

	Lender A	Lender B	Lender C	Lender D
Contact				
Product type	Business loan	Business loan	Business loan	Business loan
Personal guarantees required	Yes	No	Yes	Case by case
Financials/tax required and reviewed for the trading entity?	Yes – BAS/Financials	Yes – 2 yrs min	No	Only where ABN <2 years
Loan statements/bank feed required	12 months	12 months	6 months	
Accountant's letter in lieu of BAS/ITRs/financials	No	Yes	?	No
ABN registration	12 months	12 months	9 months	12 months

Business turnover linkage	1 month turnover	Max 3 months gross turnover, not net	1 month less fees	Yes – unknown parameters
Minimum business turnover	$10,000	$10,000 and 10 transactions	$10,000.00	?
Max loan	$250,000	$800,000	$250,000w	$150,000
Min loan	$5,000	$20,000	$5,000	$2,001
Max term	12 months	18 months	12 months	5 years
Funding turnaround time	24 hours	1 week	48 hours	24 hours
Property/other fixed asset security required	Often $200k	No	Over $50k	Yes for loans between $150k and $175k
GSA over business required	Yes	Yes	Yes	

	Lender A	Lender B	Lender C	Lender D
Interest payment timing	In advance – full term	In advance – full term	In advance	Arrears
Interest only option	No	No	No	No
Repayment cycle	Weekly	Weekly	Weekly	Monthly in arrears
Current rate range	2% to 4.5% per month	Up to 4% per month	2% to 3% per month	5% to 11% per annum
Fixed & variable rates	Fixed rates only	Fixed rates only	Fixed rates only	Variable
Estab/app fee	$1,500 or 0.25% of loan amount	1.5% comms, 0.75% resi + vals & legals	$3k	?
Acc keeping/annual fee	Loan service fees apply	Loan service fees apply	0.25% of original loan amount charged monthly in arrears	No

Early repayment/ termination fee	Yes	Yes	Yes	?
Loan purpose limitations	No unidentified working capital	No refinance	Business purpose	No
Brokerage fees included (if applicable)	Yes	Yes	Yes	Yes – capped to $445
Special conditions/ notes	Limited purpose – marketing, business expansion/ acquisition, staffing, etc	Signatory must be at least 51% shareholder. Min 10 payments per month into account. No refinance	Personal investor funds – limited appetite	Marketplace lending – reliant upon retail investors

5Cs Credit Model

Let's now have a closer look at the 5Cs Credit Model. In this model, the 5Cs of credit refer to:

1. Character
2. Capacity
3. Capital
4. Collateral
5. Conditions

When you apply for finance of any kind, the application will be subject to approval by lender credit. These criteria determine the eligibility of a loan applicant, and the related interest rate and credit limits. This process may be as simple as an automated system, or as complex as a full panel credit committee.

The result of this process determines a borrower's *creditworthiness*.

> **TOP TIP**
>
> Credit reporting has also become more comprehensive, with the ability to see credit trends over a period.

Character: What is your credit history and business experience?

The character of borrowers is coming under more and more scrutiny as technology and social platforms bring all areas of an individual's life into the open for a lender to observe.

A lender is looking for a clean credit file, with a high score showing the character of a strong borrower. Some lenders may also be looking to assess the business owner's history in directing companies and looking for any black marks against their name, such as company administration, insolvency or any other issues that may put the lender at risk of not recovering the debt.

Capacity: Do you have the capacity to repay the loan?

Capacity to service a loan is simply a calculation of the business's incomings vs its outgoings. This results in a debt-income ratio (DTI).

Assessing capacity to service the loan is quite simple, though it can be seen from three different viewpoints depending on the type of finance being applied for.

The debt-income ratio can be calculated based on company financials that are:

- Historical
- Current
- Projected/forecast

For example, a business that is generating a modest profit and has done so consistently for the last three years wants to purchase an expensive new piece of equipment that will triple its revenue with only a small increase in expenses. With a historical and current DTI ratio that is high, lenders typically shy away from finance approval due to risk. However, using twenty-four-month cash flow forecasting based on the new equipment/revenue, the business can evidence debt servicing and a lowered DTI and can easily service the new debt on top of ongoing expenses and liabilities.

Capital: How much money will you put into the transaction?

Capital is simply cash, money, or even equity that can be put into a transaction. These funds may be owned by the business owner, or the business itself in the way of retained earnings, profits in the bank or even liquid investments that can be easily cashed out.

A lender will generally want to see that the borrower has some 'skin in the game', as, when a borrower's own money is involved, it gives them a sense of responsibility and ownership, and is also an added incentive not to default on the loan.

For example, a business owner is looking to buy out a competitor with a purchase price of $1,000,000. While there is plenty of security in the transaction for the lender, they require the borrower to put up $100,000 cash as capital to reduce the risk and ensure the borrower has skin in the game.

Collateral: What assets are to be used as security for the loan?

Collateral is an asset that is used to secure a loan. Most often, the asset is the object that loan proceeds are being used to purchase, but other times it may be unrelated to the transaction or it may even be a list of many assets.

For example, a mortgage on a property is used to secure the property loan, a motor vehicle is used to secure an asset finance loan, and a General Security Agreement (GSA) can be used to secure a business loan. Collateral-backed loans are commonly known as secured loans. Thus, the lender registers an interest over the security, and in the event of a default on the loan, can take ownership of the asset and recover the losses.

The two most common forms of securing an asset are mortgages, for property and land, and the Personal Property Securities Register (PPSR), for most other assets.

Conditions: What are the conditions of the loan, the sector, and the economy?

The conditions of the loan, such as interest rate, loan-to-value ratio, length of term and borrower industry, all influence the likelihood of a lender approving a loan.

'Conditions' generally refer to how the borrower intends to use the money. Consider a borrower applying for a loan to buy a truck, a retail shop or to purchase stock. These loans will all have different conditions that will suit their purpose.

Additionally, lenders will consider the conditions outside the borrower's control, for example economic conditions, sector and industry trends or the impact of legislative or government changes.

> **TOP TIP**
>
> Business finance is a challenging sport and can get more difficult the larger and faster your business grows.

What is meant by 'lender ready'?

'Lender readiness' refers to the preparedness of a business or business owner to apply for finance to grow their business. There are many different aspects to be aware of when applying for finance for your business, and every lender will have their own unique way of analysing your information, validating the data, and processing it all for approval.

For any loan, the following general categories will be required:

- Who are you?
    - Personal identification
    - Company registration and structure
    - Trust deeds

- What are you trying to do?
    - Purchase something
    - Expand the business
    - Improve cash flow or survival

- Can you support a loan?
    - Financial records
    - Bank transactions
    - Forecasting

Depending on what you are trying to buy or do, the lender requirements can get quite detailed and might, for example, include:

- Lease agreements
- WALEs (Weighted Average Lease Expiry for tenants in a building)
- Financial models
- Feasibility studies

- Information memorandums
- Purchase orders
- Supplier agreements

Finally, there are three questions we suggest you ask yourself before any business finance application:

1. How do I translate my objectives and requirements to a lender?
2. What do I need to prepare?
3. Am I prepared for potential traps or tripwires that can halt progress?

Once you have done your homework, you should be fully prepared to navigate the lending process.

Summary

- Applying for a loan can be a lengthy process, so before you begin, ensure you are fully prepared and understand what is involved.

- Familiarising yourself with the 5Cs Credit Model will give you a head start.

- Lenders need to evaluate outside influences while assessing your loan-worthiness.

5
Sourcing Money For A Business

Now it's time to look at the last of the burning questions we asked in Chapter 3: how do I get money into the business? We looked at loans in the last chapter, but there are several other key ways to get money into a business for growth. There are some strategies, and obviously the first way is to use cash.

Cash/equity

Use your cash, or your investors' cash. This is what's generally called 'equity contribution'. Cash is also referred to as equity, and there are a couple of ways you can use cash or get cash to put into your business.

Let's see if we can expand on some of those for you.

Bootstrapping

Using your own money is often called 'bootstrapping' a business.

Perhaps you, and maybe some of your founders, put your own money into the business, which is done quite regularly to fund a business to a certain point of growth. Bootstrapping is very common, particularly in the early years of most businesses while they're proving the concept. When you get to proof of concept and proof of delivery and start looking to scale the business, however, bootstrapping often has limitations because the founders will already have put in a lot of money, and will therefore want to spread some of that risk, so they'll start seeking investment or debt finance.

Crowdfunding, or peer-to-peer finance

Crowdfunding platforms are becoming increasingly popular, and they are an effective way to allow smaller equity contributions or fractional contributions into a business. For example, instead of having $300 million to invest, or $300,000, a person might only have $300 or $3,000. Crowdfunding platforms allow for the aggregation of these smaller investments from the general public, together amounting to significant sums.

Peer-to-peer platforms effectively replace the licensed investment house or investment manager with a digital investment manager, and they allow people to invest directly into a business with smaller, fractional investments.

Essentially, with both crowdfunding and peer-to-peer finance, investors register on a platform seeking potential investment transactions. They can choose from various business categories or sectors, etc, and business owners will present their business ideas via that platform with a view to attracting investors and supporters for their business.

Grants and subsidies

Government or industry grants are often used to provide immediate financial assistance, often for research and development, innovation or job creation, even in specific industries or verticals. They are often offered in order to grow a specific industry, or part of an industry.

There are a few important things to remember about grants:

- The amount of funds available is often quite limited.
- There is usually a formal, drawn-out process for getting a grant, whether from industry or the government.
- Generally, they involve quite a detailed process and you will have to follow an application framework.
- They're hotly contested because they don't generally need repaying.

Strategic partnerships/ joint ventures

Another option is to partner with people in your industry who want to buy your client base or gain access to it, or who want to collaborate with you in some other way. Such potential partners might offer cash or they might offer to exchange clients with you so you can increase your revenue.

Joint ventures, distribution agreements, licensing deals and CO marketing campaigns are all examples of such strategic partnerships. Essentially, these partnerships allow businesses to leverage each other's resources, such as intellectual property, goodwill, customers etc.

Innovation/diversification

Diversifying your business could attract new clients and thereby bring extra revenue into your business. For example, a business that manufactures and sells hats might diversify and start selling sunglasses. Alternatively, the same business might innovate and develop an improved version of their existing hats.

This is usually a good option if you have identified an unmet need or untapped market, and you innovate or diversify in order to capitalise on the opportunity. Research and development are key here, allowing you to expand your offering and bring in more revenue to fuel business growth.

Marketing and sales

Another way in which business owners and managers can boost their revenue is by focusing on their marketing and sales efforts.

If you have a proven sales and marketing system with established conversion rates, you can effectively predict the outcome of this approach. For example, if you typically convert three out of every ten potential clients into paying customers, increasing your reach to twenty clients should, if the conversion rate stays the same, result in six conversions, effectively doubling your revenue.

Naturally, this may also increase your marketing spend, so you need to keep an eye on those numbers and look at the revenue each of your new clients brings in to make sure it remains profitable, but this is an effective way of getting money into your business at a top-line level or a revenue level.

Raising finance or capital

There are three primary forms of raising capital (money) in a business:

- Debt finance/debt
- Equity
- Convertible notes

There are other 'exotic' means of raising capital, but for the sake of simplicity, we will stick to the three above.

Debt is the most common form of raising capital as it is simple, cheap and relatively easy to achieve. Really, debt is just a loan to be repaid over a period. Equity is a bit more complex, as it involves finding investors and the selling of shares. Convertible notes are complex, as they are generally a hybrid of both debt and equity.

Let's go into each of these options in more detail.

Debt finance/debt

Debt is the most common way of injecting money into an SME business. More commonly known as a loan, debt is a legal arrangement between a lender and a borrower. The lender agrees to 'lend' the borrower a sum of money based on the 'terms' agreed with the borrower.

Some popular terms used in loan agreements are:

- Timeframe – *how long will I have to repay the loan?*
- Interest rate – *what will the interest rate be, and how is it calculated?*
- Security – *will I need to put up assets to secure the loan?*
- Repayment – *how often do I need to make repayments?*

Debt was traditionally arranged with a business banker at the bank at which you have all your business trading accounts. This provided a 'one-stop-shop' for all the products the bank has to offer and served the business space well for a long time.

More recently, however, with the advent of a plethora of smaller specialist business lenders coming onto the market, the option to use the skills of a business finance broker is becoming more and more popular, as this gives the business owner:

- One single independent relationship covering all lenders in the market
- Expertise, know-how and assistance when applying for loans
- Access to products and services from multiple lenders simultaneously
- Access to specialist lenders that only lend through the broker channel

Like a mortgage broker, the business finance broker will assist a client with the search, application, and ongoing management of a loan facility.

EXAMPLE

John is the director of DDD Trucking and has been offered a major government contract that will triple the size of his current operation. To expand, John is looking to borrow $5,000,000 to purchase a turnkey site for his business.

John's bank will not lend him enough money to complete the transaction as his current operation cannot support the new debt repayments and he doesn't have the cash reserves to put up a 35% deposit, so he contacts his finance broker for help.

FUNDING BUSINESS GROWTH

Together, they find a solution leveraging a 65% LVR first mortgage on the new property, a second mortgage over another warehouse John owns, covering the balance and including three years' interest payments.

John's business has cash reserves to cover purchase costs and associated fees.

The first mortgage is with a major bank and looks like this:

- Security: First mortgage on the new site
- Loan: $3,250,000 (65% of the asset's value)
- Term: Fifteen years (including five years interest only)
- Rate: ~3% PA = ~$8,000 per month
- The second mortgage is with a specialist lender
- Security: Second mortgage over another warehouse John already owns
- Loan: $2,275,000 ($1750,000 purchase + $525,000 interest for three years)
- Term: Three years (capitalised interest)
- Rate 10% PA

With the above, the business can move into the new site and start expanding.

Interest-only repayments provide a smooth transition, reducing cash flow burden while the company is expanding.

Capitalised interest (borrowing the interest) gives John three years to build the company up and refinance the second mortgage to a major bank.

To summarise, debts are simply a loan that is to be repaid over time, with interest. The advantages of loans are that:

- They are simple and easy to arrange
- They usually come with flexible terms
- They are available with loads of options, and there is a lot of competition in the marketplace.

Equity

Equity is the ownership of a shareholding in a business. This percentage of ownership has a monetary value. As an example, let's look at the stock market.

An individual buys $100,000 worth of shares in ABC Bank Ltd. This individual now has an equity stake in this business.

EXAMPLE

ABC Trading Ltd is looking to raise capital to expand operations into a new emerging market. To start this expansion project, they need a total of $1,000,000.

ABC Trading creates 1,000,000 new ordinary shares. ABC Trading then puts this deal into an investor offer document and sends it to their investor base hoping for a positive response.

Five investors agree to the plans, and each invests $200,000 into the business. In return they receive 200,000 shares each.

Each investor now has an equity stake in the company, owning 200,000 shares. This is a percentage of the total shares outstanding. These shareholders are also generally entitled to receive a percentage of the reported profits, based on the percentage of their equity stake.

To summarise:

- Equity is often difficult to arrange.
- It involves the sale of shares in your business, and therefore a portion of your business.

- It is potentially difficult to find and/or convince investors.
- Losing a portion of your business means losing some control.
- There are no repayments or requirements to pay back the capital.

Convertible note(s)

Let's see if we can explain convertible notes in a way that won't put you to sleep! (This is an occupational hazard, I'm afraid.)

Imagine for a moment you're a start-up company and you need some money to get your business off the ground. You could try robbing a bank, but that's probably not the best idea. Instead, you could try something called a convertible note.

A convertible note is when someone gives you a loan, but instead of paying them back with interest, you give them shares in your company. It's like borrowing money from your friend, and instead of paying them back, you give them a piece of your company. It's often a win-win situation for everyone involved – the investor gets a piece of your company, and you get the money you need to get your business off the ground.

Now, in Australia, the most common note instrument is something called a SAFE note (or Simple Agreement for Future Equity). It's slightly different to a convertible note, being that it legally isn't a debt instrument, but otherwise it is basically the same thing. With a SAFE note, instead of giving the investor shares in your company, you give them the *right to buy* shares in your company at a later date.

Convertible notes are typically used by start-ups when they're raising their first or second round of funding or when they need some 'bridge' financing between two larger rounds.

They're a great way for start-ups or scale-ups to get the money they need without having to give away too much equity in their company. Plus, they're a lot easier and quicker than going through the traditional process of raising equity funding.

To summarise:

- Convertible notes are more complex and dynamic than other ways of raising capital.

- They are a short-term instrument used to delay a dilution event (which is selling off shares in your company).

- Generally, they start as a loan and end as a shareholding (or sometimes the reverse).

Summary

- Attracting money into a business is a way of expanding that business.

- There are several options covering how and where to source money for your business.

Over the next three chapters, we will be looking at different options, case studies and examples, arming you with the skills and knowledge to use them where needed in your business.

Let's get cracking!

6
Debt Finance Products

There are many ways to structure the borrowing of money, and over time, lenders have turned these different structures into products that they can sell. Let's go through some of the most common structures available on the market, how they work, and where you can use them in your business.

First, here are some of the most common reasons why any business will require money:

- To purchase property:
    - Warehouse
    - Office
    - Land

- To purchase plant and equipment:
  - Material handling
  - Processing plant

- To purchase vehicles:
  - Trucks and trailers
  - Cars, utes or vans

- To get invoices paid early:
  - Invoice factoring
  - Invoice finance

- To purchase stock, inventory and materials:
  - Trade finance
  - Line of credit
  - Import/export

- To purchase a business:
  - Mergers
  - Acquisitions

- To pay staff, expenses and tax

When considering the purchase of an existing business in Australia, there are several finance products that can be used to facilitate the transaction. The specific product you choose will depend on various factors such as the size of your business, its financial performance, your own financial situation, and the terms offered by lenders. Let's look at some common finance products used for business purchases in Australia.

Letters of credit (LC)

Letters of credit are widely used in international trade to provide assurance to exporters that they will be paid, and to provide importers with confidence that the goods will be delivered as agreed. A letter of credit is issued by a bank on behalf of the importer and guarantees payment to the exporter upon the presentation of specified documents, such as shipping documents or invoices. For example, maybe you're trying to buy a new car from a dealership but they're not sure if they can trust you to pay for it. That's where a letter of credit comes in.

Basically, a letter of credit is like a note from your parents or a wealthy relative saying that they promise to pay for the car if you don't. Instead of your relatives, of course, it's a bank or financial institution that promises to pay the seller if you don't. It's like having a backup plan in case something goes wrong.

As another example, let's say you're a business owner and you need to buy a bunch of supplies from a supplier in another country, but you don't want to pay for the supplies until they've been shipped and you've received them. Again, this is where a letter of credit can come in handy. You can ask your bank to issue a letter of credit to the supplier, promising to pay them once the supplies have been shipped and you've received them. That way, the supplier knows they'll get paid and you know you'll get the supplies you need.

The participants in the process are:

- **The buyer (importer):** The entity purchasing the goods
- **The seller (exporter):** The entity selling and shipping the goods
- **The opening/issuing bank:** The buyer's bank that issues the letter of credit
- **The notifying/advising bank:** The seller's bank that advises the letter of credit
- **The carrier:** The transportation company delivering the goods

The following table sets out the steps in the letter of credit process.

Step	From	To	Description	Document/payment flow
1	Buyer	Seller	Signs contract	Sales contract
2	Buyer	Opening/issuing bank	Applies for L/C	Letter of credit application
3	Opening/issuing bank	Notifying/advising bank	Issue L/C	Letter of credit document
4	Notifying/advising bank	Seller	Advise	Letter of credit notification
5	Seller	Carrier	Shipping	Goods
6	Seller	Notifying/advising bank	Sends B/L	Bill of lading and shipping documents
7	Notifying/advising bank	Seller	Pay	Payment for goods
8	Notifying/advising bank	Opening/issuing bank	Sends B/L	Bill of lading and shipping documents
9	Opening/issuing bank	Notifying/advising bank	Makes payment	Payment reimbursement
10	Buyer	Opening/issuing bank	Pay and receive B/L	Payment and receipt of shipping documents
11	Buyer	Carrier	Receive goods by B/L	Goods delivery using bill of lading

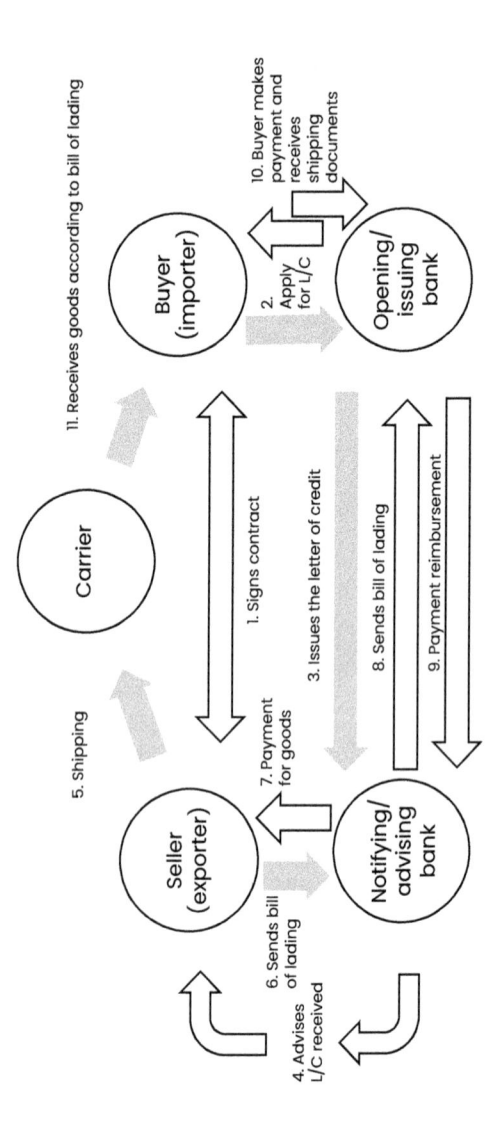

The trade finance process using a letter of credit

In the diagram, the importer is represented on the left side, the exporter is represented on the right side and the issuing bank is in the middle, connecting the two parties and providing the letter of credit. Arrows show the flow of goods, documents and payments.

So, there you have it – a letter of credit is like having a backup plan in case something goes wrong with a payment. It's essentially having your bank promise to pay for the car if you don't. And in business, it can be a great way to make sure you get what you need while also making sure everyone gets paid. Now, wasn't that funny? OK, maybe not, but hopefully it was helpful!

Venture debt and private credit

Venture debt or private credit is a type of loan that provides funding to start-up and early-stage businesses and fast-growing companies with more flexibility than other forms of debt financing. This type of financing does not require the company to give up equity in exchange for funds.

In Australia, venture debt interest rates typically range from 8% to 20% per annum. These rates are higher than those offered by banks, which typically range from 4% to 15%, but they are designed to offset the risk associated with venture lending.

This type of debt is a short- to medium-term financing solution, often lasting from one to three years. Funding strategies vary, but a common 'rule of thumb' is that a venture lender may consider a loan amount of up to 30% of the company's last equity financing round.

Venture debt can be used for various purposes, including funding working capital, acquiring assets, expanding operations and financing acquisitions. It is often used in conjunction with equity financing to help start-ups and growing companies extend their cash runway and reach key milestones without having to dilute their ownership or control.

Seller or vendor financing

Vendor or seller financing occurs when the seller of the business provides a loan to the buyer to fund a purchase. The buyer makes regular payments to the seller over an agreed-upon period (as they would with an external financier), usually with interest. Seller financing can be a viable option if traditional lenders are hesitant to finance the full amount or if the seller wants to facilitate the sale by offering favourable terms.

Offering your clients 'terms' or credit

You may work with a lender that will offer your clients credit on your behalf, so you get paid now, the lender takes a fee, and the risk is taken on by your client. You're thinking outside the box now and are contemplating being a modern-day 'Robin Hood' by offering credit to your customers. Alright, let's have some fun with this!

First things first, before giving credit, make sure your customers are worth the risk. You don't want to be stuck with a deadbeat company or client who can't keep their promise to pay you back. We therefore need to create a credit application form that includes all the details you need to know about them, like their full contact information, business structure and references. Make sure you include a legal privacy policy in the form as you can then check their background (more on this in a second).

Done? Great!

Now it's time to set the terms of credit. You can give your customers seven or twenty-one days to pay from the receipt of the original invoice, or you could simply not offer any credit terms at all.

But hold on... before you get too excited, remember that offering credit can be a bit of a gamble. That's why it's always a good idea to check the customer's credit first.

You don't want to end up with a customer who thinks 'credit' means 'free money'. Once you've got your customers' forms back, it's time to talk with a credit bureau and confirm what the clients have told you is true. (Credit bureaus are information providers that give you historical feedback on borrowers and companies in relation to payment performance and ownership.)

Now, let's put all of this into a silly example. Say you run a business that sells rare and exotic cheeses (mmm, cheese!), and a customer comes in and falls in love with your rare Gouda. They don't have enough cash on hand to buy it, but you're feeling generous so you offer them credit. You give them twenty-one days to pay from the receipt of the original invoice. But before you go handing over that Gouda, you check their credit and find out they have a history of not paying their bills on time. That's a red flag! So, you must decide whether to take the risk and give them credit or ask for payment upfront.

It's an interesting situation, but one that every business owner must face when offering credit to their customers!

Types of loan

Business acquisition loan

A business acquisition loan is specifically designed to fund the purchase of an existing business. It provides a lump sum amount to cover the purchase price, working capital and other related expenses. These loans may be secured by the business's assets, personal collateral, or a combination of both.

Commercial property loan

If the business includes real estate as part of the purchase, a commercial property loan can be used. This type of loan is secured by the property and allows you to spread the repayment over a longer term, typically up to twenty-five years. Commercial property loans are commonly used for purchasing businesses that operate in their own premises.

Government-funded small business loan

In Australia, there are similar government-backed loan programmes available, such as the Small Business Finance Corporation (SBFC) loan scheme, or loans provided by state-based development agencies. These loans are designed to support small businesses and can be used for business acquisitions. They often have favourable terms, longer repayment periods, and lower down-payment requirements.

Asset-based loan

In cases where the acquired business has valuable assets such as inventory, equipment or accounts receivable, an asset-based loan can be used. This type of loan uses the business's assets as collateral, and the loan amount is based on the appraised value of those assets. Asset-based loans can provide more flexibility in terms of loan amounts and repayment structures.

Construction loans

A construction loan is a shorter-term loan (generally six months to two-and-a-half years) and as the name implies, is used to finance the building or construction of a home or another real estate asset.

The loan is used to cover the costs of the project (purchase of the land, construction materials, tradesmen, and project professionals) before obtaining long-term funding once the building project is complete. Construction loans are relatively risky in the eyes of lenders as there are more variables or risks than a traditional loan (for a built property, for example)

The length of a construction loan is generally linked directly to the construction contract that it is being used to finance. For example, if the construction contract is estimated to take nine months, the loan term would often be twelve months – nine months for construction, plus a little bit of leeway for time overruns, plus some time to refinance to a normal loan once the building is complete.

With a traditional property loan, the borrower pays the interest (and, depending on the setup of the loan, the loan principle). With a construction loan, the borrowers will often be allowed to add part of all the loan interest to the loan itself and start making payments once construction is completed.

In terms of getting the loan approved, there is a little more complexity involved than normal. Lenders will often want to vet the builder for their experience and make sure they have enough working capital to complete the job. Lenders will also often have an independent third party (such as a quantity surveyor) validate the costings quoted in the construction contract to make sure they are reasonable.

Staged payments are made by the lender in milestones that are agreed in writing by all parties and often checked and measured by the lender before the release of funds.

DEBT FINANCE PRODUCTS

Builders generally need to be qualified and independent of the borrower.

Some lenders offer 'owner – builder' construction loans, but they are few and far between and generally only apply if the borrower is a licensed builder.

There are some important considerations to bear in mind with construction loans:

- It can be tricky to co-ordinate all the lender requirements, the project professionals and timings.

- Construction contracts can be 'fixed price' or 'cost plus an agreed margin' for the builder (Cost +). Builders don't like fixed price as they can get stuck with building cost overruns for unexpected issues. Lenders don't like 'Cost +' as they only lend a defined amount. You can't build without money, so most contracts financed are fixed price at higher prices to cover potential issues.

- Your deposit goes in first – the lender works on a 'cost to complete' basis. For example, if your land and build cost

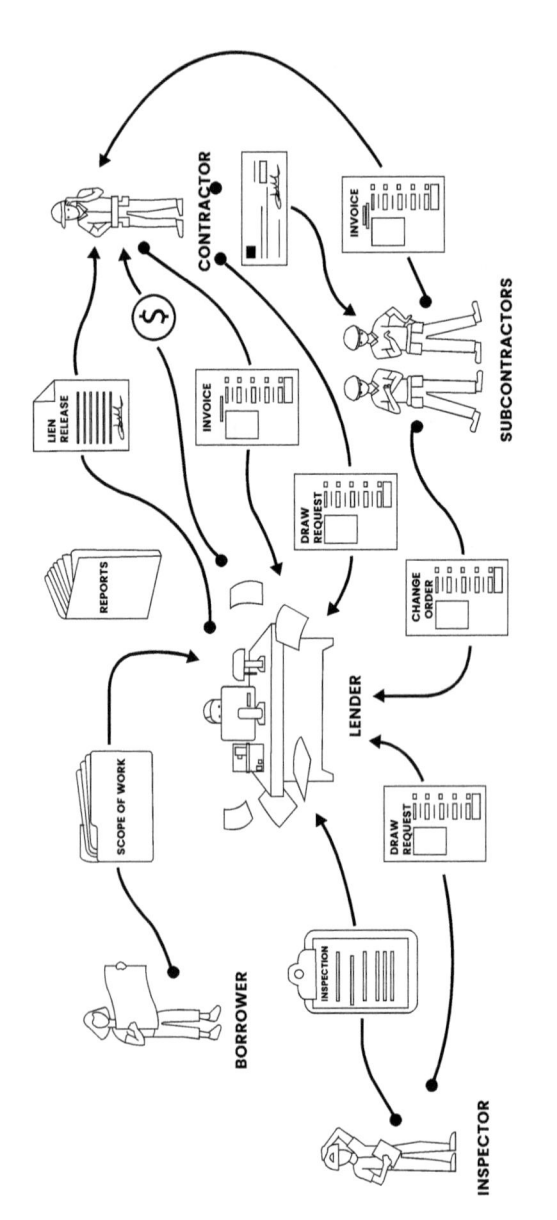

Construction loans

was $500k and the lender is loaning you 80% ($400k of the accepted build cost), you would need to put in the last $100k before the lender will advance funds. Once you have done that, the lender will confirm there is only $400k required to complete the build. If the cost has risen and it is now $450k, you would need to put in another $50k before they will advance the loan.

EXAMPLE

Georgina wants to have a new house built for a total of $500,000. The land purchase cost is $150,000 and the building construction cost is approximately $300,000. Other costs (professional fees, consultants and allowances) are around $50,000. The total development cost is therefore $500,000.

At the start of the build, the 'cost to complete' would be $500k, therefore Georgina needs to contribute $100k of her own cash (or other equity) so that the remaining cost to complete is the same as the approved loan amount (which is $400k).

In the first month, only $50,000 is required to cover costs, so Georgina takes only that amount – and pays interest only on that amount, saving her money.

Georgina continues to take funds as they are needed, guided by the drawdown schedule.

She pays interest only on the total that she has drawn down rather than paying interest on the whole $500,000 for the entire term of the loan.

At the end of the year, she refinances with her local bank the total amount of funds she has used into a term loan or line of credit mortgage for the longer term.

Term loans

Term loans are often used for a variety of worthwhile business and/or personal uses, generally to accumulate personal or business assets. These include residential, commercial, land or industrial property purchases, business working capital, business or personal assets, or plant, equipment and car purchases. With a traditional term loan, the borrower pays the interest (and, depending on the setup of the loan, the loan principal, from the outset or after one to five years until the end of the loan).

DEBT FINANCE PRODUCTS

There are some important considerations with term loans:

- Generally, they are 'set and forget' – once set up, they are hard to change without starting a new application from scratch.
- Ideally, you need to match the term to the life of the corresponding asset.
- They are single drawdown only. Redrawing on the loan principal you have repaid isn't always possible.
- They are not normally available for construction projects.

EXAMPLE

Tony wants to buy a 30-year-old house in Melbourne, Australia, for a total of $900,000.

A term loan is approved for 80% of the property's value – $720,000.

Purchase costs such as stamp duty, removals, legal fees etc add up to around 5% of the total purchase cost of the property, which is therefore estimated to be $945,000.

- Tony puts in cash/equity of $225,000, which is the balance between the loan and the total cost of the purchase.

- The loan of $720,000 draws down with a term of thirty years.
  - Tony pays interest of 5% per annum, which is $36,000 for the first five years.
  - From year six to year thirty, Tony also pays down the principle of $28,800 per annum in addition to any interest on the amount outstanding.
  - The interest payable will reduce as the loan is paid down.

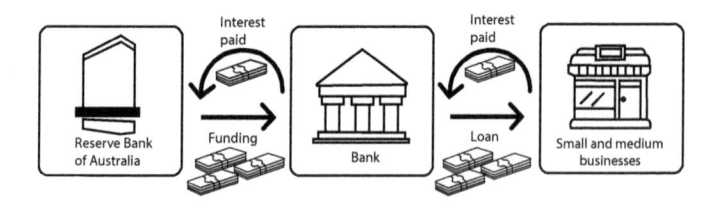

The term loans process

Other options: Trade finance and import-export finance

Trade finance is a method used by businesses to facilitate the import and export of goods. It is used to provide funding and financial guarantees to support the purchase and sale of goods, and to manage the associated

DEBT FINANCE PRODUCTS

risks. It is important for businesses engaged in import–export activities to understand their financing needs and explore the various finance products available. Consider the specific requirements of your trade transactions, the creditworthiness of your trading partners, and the associated risks.

There are several different types of trade finance, which we're going to look at here.

One common example of trade finance is the use of a letter of credit, which we looked at right at the start of the chapter. Another is import–export finance.

Import–export finance is a specialised form of financing that helps businesses that are engaged in international trade to manage their cash flow and mitigate the risks associated with cross-border transactions. It provides the necessary funds to facilitate the import or export of goods and helps bridge the gap between the time that goods are shipped and the time that payment is received. Here are some key finance products used in import–export finance.

Export credit insurance

Export credit insurance protects exporters against the risk of nonpayment by foreign buyers. It provides coverage for commercial and political risks, such as buyer default, insolvency or political instability. Export credit insurance enables exporters to expand their sales to new markets and improve their access to financing by mitigating the risk of nonpayment.

Export factoring

Export factoring is a financing arrangement where a finance company purchases an exporter's accounts receivable at a discounted rate, providing immediate cash flow. The factor assumes the credit risk associated with the receivables and collects payments from the importer. Export factoring can help businesses improve their cash flow and reduce the risk of nonpayment.

Export working capital programmes

Various government agencies, such as export-import banks or trade finance organisations, offer export working capital programmes to support businesses engaged in export activities. These programmes provide financing options tailored to exporters, including working capital loans, loan guarantees or credit enhancements.

Supply chain financing

Supply chain financing, also known as reverse factoring, is a finance product that allows businesses to optimise their cash flow by providing early payment to suppliers. In these arrangements, the importer's bank pays the supplier on behalf of the importer, and the importer repays the bank later. Supply chain financing improves the financial health of the entire supply chain by providing working capital to suppliers and extending payment terms for importers.

Summary

- Construction loans are more work to manage over the term than standard loans, and as such often attract higher setup and ongoing fees as well as higher interest rates.

- A term loan is a longer-term loan (generally, one to forty years) and, as the name implies, is used to pay off an asset over a longer term.

- Trade finance loans provide short-term financing to cover the working capital needs of importers and exporters. These loans can be used to fund the purchase of goods, manage cash flow, or meet other trade-related expenses. Trade finance loans may be secured by the underlying goods, receivables or other collateral.

- Consult with banks, specialised trade finance institutions and professional advisors with expertise in import–export finance to determine the most suitable finance products for your international trade operations.

7
Specialised Funding, Ownership And IP

The most common finance methods when buying physical business assets such as equipment are listed below. The type is generally determined by its purpose, tax treatment and/or the type of business:

- Chattel mortgage (a loan you pay off over a term)

- Operating lease (a lease you pay over a term)

- Rental lease (a rental agreement for the vehicle)

It is important to evaluate each finance product carefully, considering factors such as interest rates, repayment terms, collateral requirements and any associated fees. Consult with financial advisors, lenders or business acquisition specialists in Australia to determine the most suitable finance product for your specific situation. Conduct thorough due diligence on the business you intend to purchase to ensure its financial viability and growth potential within the Australian market.

Two examples of application types are given below – a full application vs a streamlined application with a lender that specialises in asset finance.

Full application (typically to a major bank)

Collateral	The business being purchased
Capacity	Company financial statements, assets and liabilities etc
Character	Comprehensive credit check, time trading and trade reference check
Capital	0–30% deposit[2]

---

[2] Deposits are generally required where the borrower is not a property owner, the asset is considered exotic or there is a lower credit score (therefore a higher risk of default).

Conditions	One to seven years
Balloon	10–30%[3]
Percentage rates	Market leading[4]
Average time to settle	One to two weeks

*Streamlined or LowDoc application
(specialised asset finance lender)*

Collateral	The business being purchased
Capacity	Self-declared income
Character	Basic credit check and time trading
Capital	0–30% deposit
Conditions	Three to five years
Balloon	10–30%
Percentage rates	Around 0–3% over market
Average time to settle	Twenty-four to seventy-two hours

---

3 A balloon or a residual is a lump sum payment made at the end of the loan contract. Typically, this is 10–30% of the asset's value at purchase. This payment reduces the monthly repayments – eg a business purchaser can use a balloon to align repayments with business cash flow.

4 The market rate for business finance fluctuates and therefore is not printed here. It is roughly aligned with the average residential home lending rate at any point in time.

FUNDING BUSINESS GROWTH

Fuelling growth in the building industry

In the construction and development sector, funding plays a vital role in bringing projects to life. This section explores how construction and development finance works, providing a clear understanding of this specialised form of funding.

Construction and development finance is a tailored solution for building projects. It involves financing released in stages to align with project progress. Here's a simple explanation of these stages:

- **Project assessment:** Present a project plan to the lender, including scope, cost estimates, timelines and potential returns. The lender evaluates viability and risk before approving funding.

- **Loan agreement:** Enter into a loan agreement with the lender, outlining terms, interest rates and repayment schedules.

- **Stage-based funding:** Finance is released in stages corresponding to project milestones. Funds cover construction costs and related expenses.

- **Valuations and certifications:** Periodic valuations ensure loan amounts align with market value and project progress. Certifications from professionals validate completion and quality of work.

- **Interest payments and repayment:** Make interest-only payments during construction. Transition to regular repayments once the project is complete.

- **Contingency funds:** Set aside a contingency fund for unforeseen expenses.

Construction and development finance offers the following advantages for building businesses:

- **Tailored funding:** Designed specifically for construction projects, considering cash flow needs and risks.

- **Flexible drawdowns:** Stage-based funding provides flexibility, reducing financing costs.

- **Risk mitigation:** Thorough project assessments identify risks, benefiting both borrower and lender.

- **Expertise and support:** Lenders with industry experience offer guidance and support.

Construction and development finance supports the unique needs of building projects. By providing stage-based funding, flexibility and risk mitigation, this finance empowers builders to undertake projects and drive business growth. Understanding construction and development finance is crucial for securing the necessary funds. Work with reputable lenders experienced in this area to achieve success in the dynamic construction industry.

Invoice financing

Invoice financing is a powerful tool that empowers businesses to unlock the value of their unpaid invoices, providing immediate access to cash flow for growth and expansion. By using invoice finance, you can bridge the gap between invoice issuance and payment, optimise your cash flow, and focus on driving your business forward.

Imagine you have provided goods or services to a customer and have issued an invoice with payment terms of thirty days. Instead of waiting for the customer to pay, you can use invoice finance to access a portion of the invoice value upfront. Here's how it typically works:

1. **Issue the invoice:** You provide your goods or services to your customer and issue an invoice with the agreed payment terms.

2. **Invoice submission:** You submit the invoice to an invoice finance provider, such as a bank or a specialised finance company. They verify the authenticity of the invoice and assess the creditworthiness of your customer.

3. **Funding advance:** Upon approval, the invoice finance provider advances you a percentage (typically 70–90%) of the invoice value, providing immediate cash flow to your business. This allows you to bridge the gap between delivering the goods or services and receiving payment.

4. **Collection and payment:** The invoice finance provider takes on the responsibility of collecting payment from your customer when the invoice falls due. They may handle the entire collections process, or work in collaboration with you, depending on the type of invoice finance arrangement.

5. **Final payment:** Once your customer pays the invoice in full, the invoice finance provider releases the remaining portion of the invoice value to you, minus any fees or charges agreed upon.

Invoice finance offers several benefits that can help your business thrive:

- **Improved cash flow:** By accessing funds tied up in unpaid invoices, you can address immediate financial needs, pay suppliers, meet payroll and invest in growth opportunities without waiting for payment.

- **Flexibility:** Invoice finance is a flexible financing solution that can grow with your business. The amount of funding available to you increases as your sales and invoicing volume grows, making it suitable for businesses of various sizes.

- **Reduced credit risk:** Invoice finance providers typically assess the creditworthiness of your customers before approving funding, helping to minimise the risk of nonpayment. This provides added security for your business.

- **Time and cost savings:** Outsourcing the collections process to the invoice finance provider saves you time and resources, allowing you to focus on core business operations. Additionally, invoice finance may eliminate the need for costly overdrafts or expensive short-term loans.

Considerations

As a business owner seeking to fuel growth, there are several things you need to consider to make yourself more attractive to lenders and protect your business. Let's look at some of the most important.

Ownership of assets and lending

Being able to provide proof of ownership of the assets you are pledging is a critical requirement for lenders. Demonstrating clear ownership, or 'title', gives lenders confidence by providing assurance that the assets can be pledged as collateral to contribute to the overall financial health of the business.

By maintaining accurate records, registering and protecting intellectual property, obtaining professional valuations, preserving a clear chain of title and engaging legal counsel, businesses can effectively establish ownership and provide the necessary evidence to instil confidence in lenders. Demonstrating ownership increases the chances of securing financing, leveraging assets as collateral, and fuelling sustainable growth and expansion.

Various strategies and documentation methods can be used by businesses to effectively establish ownership and maximise their chances of securing lending opportunities. Let's have a look at some of them now.

Maintain accurate and updated records

Keep records around ownership of assets. This includes detailed documentation of purchase agreements, invoices, receipts and titles or deeds for major assets such as real estate, equipment, vehicles and intellectual property.

By keeping comprehensive records, you create a trail of evidence that supports your claim of ownership and helps speed up the due diligence process conducted by incoming lenders.

Register and protect intellectual property

Often a part of a business's value is its intellectual property, or IP. For businesses that possess valuable intellectual property, such as patents, trademarks, or copyrights, it's important that they can clearly demonstrate their ownership of that IP and that it is properly registered in order for their value to be protected.

Intellectual property rights are recognised legal forms of ownership and can significantly enhance your borrowing capacity.

> **TOP TIP**
>
> Registering your IP with the appropriate governmental agencies not only establishes your ownership, but also provides an added layer of protection against infringement.

Lenders view well-protected intellectual property as an asset, which can positively impact lending decisions.

Obtain professional third-party valuations

When dealing with high-value assets, such as real estate, machinery and inventory, obtaining professional valuations can strengthen your position as the rightful owner. Engage certified appraisers or valuation experts who can not only provide objective assessments of the assets' market value, but also serve as independent verifiers of your ownership of the asset. This verification provides lenders with greater comfort regarding the assets' value as collateral.

Maintain a clear chain of title

For assets with a chain of ownership, such as real estate, it is vital to maintain a clear and unbroken chain of title. This means conducting thorough title searches to ensure there are no liens, encumbrances or disputes that could challenge your ownership rights. Any inconsistencies or unresolved issues in the chain of title can raise concerns for lenders, potentially impacting their willingness to extend financing. Seeking legal assistance to ensure a clean and clear chain of title is essential for demonstrating ownership.

Engage legal counsel

Navigating the complexities of asset ownership and lending often necessitates the expertise of legal professionals.

> **TOP TIP**
>
> Working with legal counsel ensures that your business is well-prepared and equipped to provide the necessary evidence of ownership to lenders.

Engage experienced attorneys specialising in commercial law to provide guidance and ensure compliance with legal requirements. They can review contracts, assess ownership documentation, and offer advice on strengthening your ownership claims.

Summary

- Consider exploring invoice finance options with reputable providers to harness the benefits of this financing solution and propel your business growth to new heights.

- Intellectual property is a valuable part of your business.
- Proving ownership of assets is a crucial step when seeking lending opportunities for business growth.

PART THREE
FUND

You've decided that you want to grow your business through funding, now let's take a look at how you navigate the loan process, the options available, and how to ensure the best outcome.

8
Who Will Lend Me Money?

For most business owners, this is a simple yet often flawed decision. 'I'm going to speak to my bank,' you might decide, the thinking being, 'The bank has stood by us for years, providing a safe place to save money, offering us our first credit card, vehicle loan, home loan and now an overdraft. They have always looked after me so I will always be loyal to them.'

> **TOP TIP**
>
> While large banks generally provide a great service to their customers, the primary objective of the lender is to make money for its shareholders. Servicing their small, loyal customers is unlikely to be an important topic in the boardroom.

When you go shopping for a small item, you generally look out for the best deal, quality of service and a product that matches exactly your needs and objectives. Would it make sense to also take this methodology and apply it to your business finance decisions?

Absolutely.

Now let's see how we can broaden the panel of potential lenders available to you.

Private lenders

Private lenders are simply private entities that lend money to businesses. They typically have access to a pool of funds, whether that is in-house or via investors. Like the other nonbank lenders, they do not take deposits and are therefore free to operate on an open market. Private lenders rarely advertise their services, and therefore the introduction is usually made by a finance broker, lawyer or accountant. The products on offer are typically simpler than banks or specialist lenders, who have sophisticated software to originate and manage complex facilities.

Private lenders generally lend in the following spaces:

- Property – borrowing to purchase property
- Assets – borrowing to purchase plant, equipment, vehicle, and other business assets
- Acquisitions – borrowing to purchase a business

There are a number of pros and cons to using a private lender.

Pros	Cons
• Speed of execution	• High entry costs
• Simplicity	• High interest rates
• Flexibility	• Difficult to find

A bank of other potential lenders

Aside from private lenders, there is a wide range of other potential lenders you might consider:

- **Online lenders:** Online lenders have emerged as an alternative to traditional banks. They offer quick and convenient access to funding with less stringent eligibility criteria. Online lenders use technology to streamline the loan application and approval process.

- **Peer-to-peer (P2P) lending:** P2P lending platforms connect individual investors with borrowers, eliminating the need for traditional financial institutions. Borrowers create loan listings, and investors can choose to fund those listings based on their risk appetite and return expectations.

- **Angel investors:** Angel investors are individuals or groups who invest their own capital in promising businesses in exchange for equity ownership. They often provide not only funding, but valuable expertise and guidance as well.

- **Venture capitalists (VCs):** Venture capital firms invest in high-growth businesses in exchange for equity. They typically focus on start-ups and early-stage companies with significant growth potential.

- **Crowdfunding:** Crowdfunding platforms allow businesses to raise funds from many individuals, usually in exchange for a product, service or equity. It is essential to carefully plan and execute a compelling crowdfunding campaign to attract potential investors.

- **Grants and government programmes:** Research grants and government programmes provide funding for specific industries, projects or targeted demographics. These programmes can offer financial assistance without the need for repayment.

- **Friends and family:** In some cases, entrepreneurs turn to their personal network for financial support. Borrowing from friends and family can provide flexibility and convenience, but it's important to establish clear terms and maintain professionalism in the borrowing relationship.

Who else will lend me money?

Industry specialist lenders

This is a category of lender that differs distinctly from banks – while they are financial institutions, they do not have a deposit-taking function, only lending money. This gives them a more focused approach to the way they do business and removes a lot of the regulatory compliance that a deposit-taking institution must work with.

Specialist lenders have been around for a long time, and traditionally focused on basic asset and factoring-style finance facilities, however the sector has exploded in recent years thanks to the advent of financial technology giving birth to new finance facilities and a myriad of lenders offering pretty much anything you can imagine.

Most specialist lenders have niche structured finance products to help them stand out from the pack, and generally work tightly with finance brokers to ensure the best client experience. They are typically run for-profit and for the benefit of their shareholders. Some example categories of specialist lenders and their uses include:

- **Asset:** Borrowing to purchase plant, equipment, vehicles and other business assets.

- **Invoice/debtor:** Borrowing against outstanding invoices.

- **Trade/supplier:** Borrowing to purchase inventory or pay suppliers.

- **Property:** Borrowing to purchase property.

There are a number of advantages and disadvantages to using industry specialist lenders.

Pros	Cons
• Delivery speed	• Slightly more expensive than major banks
• Simplicity	• No branch networks
• Expertise	• Harder to find

Banks and credit unions

Banks or credit unions are the most popular place for many borrowers to start when looking to borrow money. Not only do they feel safe and secure, they also will likely have a branch nearby where you can drop in and talk to a human.

Put simply, a bank or credit union is a financial institution that takes deposits and makes loans. They also provide a vast array of auxiliary services outside the scope of this book.

Traditionally, the deposits on a bank's balance sheet were used to lend out to borrowers. Banks are generally companies run for-profit and for the benefit of their shareholders. There are various types of banks, often operating in different areas with different uses:

- **Retail banks:** Service the public and SMEs
- **Investment banks:** Specialise in corporate and institutional clients, and dealing with mergers and acquisitions etc
- **Commercial bank:** Retail banking for larger businesses
- **Credit unions:** Service the public, and are generally nonprofit
- **Central banks:** Nonmarket-based banks, responsible for currency stability, inflation and national monetary policies

As with other options explored in this chapter, there are a number of advantages and disadvantages with banks and credit unions:

Pros
- Good interest rates
- Safe and secure
- Usually have a network of branches

Cons
- Slower
- Bureaucratic, with a lot of red tape
- Inflexible

Summary

- Each funding option has its own requirements, benefits and considerations.
- It is crucial to thoroughly research and evaluate each option based on your business's needs, stage and financial situation.
- Consider consulting with a financial advisor or business mentor to help you navigate the process and make informed decisions.

9
Ticking The Boxes

Getting the right advice before applying for a loan is important to ensure that you fully understand the loan terms, repayment requirements and potential risks. Here are some tips for getting the right advice:

- **Engage a finance broker:** The services of an industry-accredited finance broker are vital in the modern lending landscape.

- **Research the loan:** Before applying for a loan, do your research to understand the loan product, the lender's requirements and the potential costs and risks associated with the loan. Seek advice from financial advisors and accountants to ensure that all tax and planning implications are known before taking out the loan.

- **Ask questions:** Don't be afraid to ask questions and clarify any doubts or uncertainties you may have about the loan terms or requirements.

- **Read the fine print:** Make sure you read the loan contract carefully and understand all the terms and conditions, including the interest rate, repayment terms, fees and any penalties for late payments or default.

- **Compare loan offers:** Shop around and compare loan offers from multiple lenders to ensure you're getting the best terms and rates.

In general, better information can lead to cheaper loan rates because it reduces the lender's risk and uncertainty. When a lender has more information about a borrower's creditworthiness, financial history and ability to repay the loan, they can more accurately assess their risk and determine an appropriate interest rate.

For example, if a borrower has a good credit score and a strong financial history, the lender may consider them a low risk and offer a lower interest rate. On the other hand, if a borrower has a poor credit history or a high level of debt, the lender may view them as a higher risk and charge a higher interest rate to compensate for that risk.

> **TOP TIP**
>
> Providing more information or documentation may also help borrowers qualify for certain loan programmes or incentives that offer lower interest rates or fees.

Although providing better information can lead to better loan terms and rates, it's important to keep in mind that lenders will also consider other factors such as the loan amount, repayment terms and collateral when determining the interest rate. It's always a good idea to shop around and compare loan offers from different lenders to ensure you're getting the best rate possible.

Supporting a loan

Whether your business can support a loan depends on various factors, such as your business's financial history, creditworthiness and ability to repay the loan. Here are some factors that lenders may consider when assessing your business's ability to support a loan:

- **Credit history:** Lenders will review your business's credit history to see if you have a track record of repaying debts on time. A good credit history can increase your chances of being approved for a loan.

- **Financial statements:** Lenders will review your business's financial statements, including income statements, balance sheets and cash flow statements, to assess your financial health and ability to repay the loan.

- **Collateral:** If you are applying for a secured loan, the lender may require collateral, such as property, equipment or inventory, to secure the loan. The value of the collateral will be considered when assessing your ability to support the loan.

- **Business plan:** Lenders may also review your business plan to assess your management and marketing strategies, as well as your projections for future growth and revenue.

- **Industry and market conditions:** Lenders may consider the overall economic conditions of your industry and market, as well as any potential risks or challenges that could affect your ability to repay the loan.

Overall, whether your business can support a loan will depend on a combination of these factors and others specific to your business and the lender's requirements. It's important to carefully assess your financial situation and explore your lending options before applying for a loan.

Tax management for business growth and lending success

Here are a few simple tips to keep your business looking squeaky clean for the tax man.

- Run a cash flow forecast for the next twenty-four months (do this annually with the accountant, or if the business changes strategy).

- Estimate the tax obligations on a quarterly or monthly basis.
- Accrue these assumed tax obligations into a separate account so they can be paid when due.

As your business experiences years of robust revenue and soaring profits, you might naturally contemplate growth and expansion. However, when seeking financing, one crucial aspect that lenders prioritise is your company's tax position, as well as the tax position of its directors. In this section, we delve into the significance of a favourable tax position, explain why lenders care about it, and provide practical strategies to improve and maintain it. By implementing these steps, you can not only enhance your business's operations, but also increase your chances of securing lending opportunities for sustainable growth.

Understanding the importance of a favourable tax position

The tax position of your business offers lenders valuable insights into your overall financial management and the state of your governance, and a favourable tax position demonstrates that your business is well-managed and has a strong understanding of its financial responsibilities. While it is true that everyone must pay taxes, a tax liability can indicate that a business has not adequately accounted for its ongoing tax obligations. Lenders seek businesses with a track record of fulfilling their tax obligations promptly and efficiently, as it reflects the organisation's fiscal discipline and reliability. Conversely, a tax liability raises concerns about financial management capabilities and the potential risks associated with lending to your business.

There are several strategies you can use to improve your tax position:

- **Conduct a comprehensive cash flow forecast:** Working closely with your accountant, establish a cash flow forecast for the next twelve to twenty-four months, reassessing it annually or whenever significant changes occur in your business strategy. By forecasting your cash flow, you can better estimate your tax obligations on a quarterly or monthly basis. This proactive approach allows you to plan, ensuring the availability of funds for timely tax payments.

- **Accurately estimate your tax obligations:** Within your cash flow forecast, diligently estimate your tax obligations to gain a clear understanding of your financial responsibilities. Consider factors such as income tax, payroll taxes, sales tax and any other applicable taxes specific to your business. This estimation helps you allocate resources and anticipate your tax liabilities, ensuring you have adequate funds set aside for timely payments.

- **Establish a separate tax obligations account:** To maintain financial discipline and meet your tax obligations promptly, create a separate account dedicated to accruing funds for tax payments. By segregating these funds, you minimise the risk of diverting them for other purposes, ensuring they are readily available when due. This practice not only simplifies tax payment processes but also establishes a transparent financial system that showcases your responsible financial management to lenders.

- **Engage with tax professionals:** Collaborating with experienced tax professionals, such as accountants or tax advisors, can significantly benefit your business. They possess in-depth knowledge of tax laws, regulations and optimisation strategies specific to your industry. Their expertise will enable you to stay compliant with tax requirements, identify potential deductions or incentives, and make informed decisions that positively impact your tax position.

Developing and maintaining a favourable tax position is essential for businesses aiming to secure financing and achieve sustainable growth. By implementing strategies such as conducting cash flow forecasts, accurately estimating tax obligations, and establishing a dedicated tax obligations account, you can showcase responsible financial management to lenders.

Seek guidance from tax professionals to ensure you stay up to date with your tax regulations and take advantage of any opportunities to optimise your tax position.

Summary

- Applying for a loan is a serious financial decision and should be approached with care and caution.

- Take the time to do your research, seek advice and ask questions so you are better able to make an informed decision and avoid potential financial pitfalls.

- Maintain a squeaky-clean tax position to not only enhance your business's operational efficiency, but also increase your chances of accessing vital funding for expansion and achieving long-term success.

10
The Loan Process: Navigating The Final Stages

Once you have gathered and organised all the necessary data and documentation for your loan application, the next step is to submit it to lenders. The lender submission stage is a critical part of the loan process, as it determines whether your application will proceed to the evaluation and approval phase. Here are the key considerations and best practices for submitting your loan application to lenders:

- **Research and identify potential lenders:** Before submitting your loan application, conduct thorough research to identify lenders that align with your financing needs and business requirements. Consider factors such as loan types, interest rates, repayment terms and eligibility criteria. Compare different lenders to find those who specialise in your industry or have experience working with businesses like yours.

- **Prepare a comprehensive loan application package:** A well-prepared loan application package increases your chances of securing financing. Include all the required documents and information discussed in the previous section, such as personal and business information, financial statements, tax returns, bank statements, credit reports, your business plan, collateral documentation and legal and regulatory documents. Ensure that the application is organised, accurate and complete to present a professional and thorough representation of your business.

- **Follow the lender's guidelines and instructions:** Each lender will have specific guidelines and instructions for submitting loan applications. Pay close attention to these requirements and adhere to them meticulously. This may include completing specific forms, providing additional documents, or following a specific submission format. Failing to comply with the lender's instructions could result in delays or even rejection of your application.

- **Craft a persuasive loan proposal:** Accompany your loan application with a well-written loan proposal that highlights the key aspects of your business and loan request. Your loan proposal should articulate your objectives, explain how the funds will be used, showcase your business's financial viability, and outline your repayment plan. Clearly communicate the potential benefits for the lender and demonstrate your ability to generate sufficient cash flow to meet repayment obligations.

> **TOP TIP**
>
> The more information you provide to support the upside and mitigate or reduce the risk of any downside with your loan application, the better your rates, fees and loan terms will be.

Once your loan application has been approved and the lender has communicated their intent to provide financing, the loan documents and settlement stage comes into play. This stage involves the preparation, review and signing of the necessary loan documents, followed by the settlement process in which the funds are disbursed. In this section, we will explore the key aspects of loan documents and settlement to help you navigate the final stages of securing your loan for business growth.

Loan document preparation

Upon loan approval, the lender will provide you with a set of documents that outline the terms and conditions of the loan. These documents may include a promissory note, a loan agreement, a security agreement (if applicable), and any other supporting documents specific to your loan type. Review these documents carefully and seek legal advice if necessary to ensure that you fully understand the terms and obligations. Here's a step-by-step guide through this process:

- **Review the loan terms and conditions:** Before signing any loan document, thoroughly review the terms and conditions outlined within. Pay close attention to the interest rate, repayment schedule, late payment penalties, prepayment penalties (if applicable), and any other fees or charges associated with the loan.

- **Seek professional guidance:** Consider consulting with an attorney or a financial advisor who specialises in loan agreements. They can help you understand the legal implications of the loan documents, identify any potential risks or unfavourable clauses, and provide guidance on negotiating certain terms if necessary. Their expertise can help protect your interests and ensure that you are making informed decisions.

- **Execute the loan documents:** Once you are satisfied with the terms of the loan and have addressed any concerns or negotiations, it's time to execute the loan documents. Ensure that all parties involved, including yourself and the lender, sign the documents as required. Keep copies of the fully executed loan documents for your records.

- **Begin the loan settlement process:** After the loan documents have been executed, the settlement process begins. This involves the disbursement of the loan funds to your designated account. The lender may require certain conditions to be met before releasing the funds, such as providing proof of insurance or additional documentation. Fulfil these conditions promptly to facilitate a smooth settlement process.

- **Monitor and repay:** Once the loan settlement is complete, it is essential to diligently track and manage your loan repayment obligations. Set up a system to ensure timely repayments, including reminders or automated transfers. Maintain open communication with the lender and promptly address any issues or concerns that may arise during the repayment period.

> **TOP TIP**
>
> Ensure that the terms of your loan align with what you have discussed previously with the lender and agreed upon during the application process.

Document storage and record-keeping

Organise and store safely all loan documents, including the fully executed agreements, receipts and other related correspondence. Maintain an accurate record of your loan transactions, repayment history and any changes or modifications made to the loan terms over time. This documentation will be valuable for future reference and may be required for audits or financial reporting purposes.

The loan documents and settlement stage mark the final steps in securing your loan for business growth. Thoroughly review and understand the loan terms and conditions before signing any document.

Facilitate a smooth settlement process by fulfilling any outstanding conditions and monitor your repayment obligations diligently. Maintain proper documentation and record-keeping to support future reporting requirements. By navigating these final stages effectively, you can proceed with confidence in achieving your business growth objectives.

Loan approval conditions: Understanding the requirements

After submitting your loan application, the lender evaluates it to determine whether to approve or decline the loan. Loan approval conditions refer to the specific requirements and conditions that must be met for the loan to be approved. Now let's explore the common approval conditions imposed by lenders and provide guidance on how to navigate them effectively:

- **Creditworthiness assessment:** Lenders assess your creditworthiness to evaluate the risk associated with lending to your business. Approval conditions related to creditworthiness may include a minimum credit score requirement, a review of your credit history, and an assessment of your debt-to-income ratio. It is important to maintain a strong credit profile and address any negative factors that could affect your loan approval.

- **Collateral evaluation:** For secured loans, lenders may require collateral. Approval conditions related to collateral evaluation involve assessing the value, ownership and marketability of the proposed collateral. Lenders want to be sure that the collateral provides sufficient security for the loan amount. Ensure that you have accurate documentation and information about the collateral and its value to satisfy these conditions.

- **Financial capacity and stability:** Lenders will examine your financial capacity and stability to determine whether you can comfortably repay the loan. They may want to assess your income, cash flow, profitability and overall financial health. Lenders want to ensure that your business generates sufficient revenue and can meet the loan repayment obligations. Prepare comprehensive financial statements and provide evidence of stable income and cash flow to satisfy these conditions.

- **Business plan assessment:** Lenders often evaluate the viability and potential of your business by looking at your business plan. They will review your plan to assess your industry knowledge, growth strategies, competitive advantages and market opportunities. Ensure that your business plan is well-crafted, demonstrates a clear path for growth, and aligns with the lender's requirements to meet these conditions.

- **Document verification:** Lenders may require additional document verification as an approval condition. This can include verifying your identity, business registration, licences, permits, contracts and other legal and regulatory documents. Ensure that all the submitted documentation is accurate, up to date, and can withstand verification to meet these conditions.

- **Repayment and loan terms:** Approval conditions related to loan repayment and terms involve reviewing your proposed repayment plan, loan term and interest rates. Lenders will assess your ability to make regular loan payments within the specified terms. Ensure that your repayment plan is realistic, based on your financial projections, and aligns with the lender's requirements.

- **Compliance with legal and regulatory requirements:** Lenders may impose approval conditions that relate to complying with legal and regulatory requirements. This may include ensuring that your business is operating within the applicable laws and regulations of your industry. Compliance with tax obligations, environmental regulations, employment laws and other legal requirements may also be assessed by the lender. Ensure that your business is in good standing and adheres to all relevant legal and regulatory obligations to meet these conditions.

Understanding and fulfilling the lender's approval conditions is crucial. Take the time to review the specific conditions imposed by lenders and ensure that you meet their requirements. To recap the most important points: maintain a strong credit profile, provide accurate documentation, demonstrate financial stability, present a solid business plan, and comply with your legal and regulatory obligations.

Maintain communication and follow up

After submitting your loan application, maintain open lines of communication with the lender. Stay responsive and promptly address any additional information or documentation requests they may make. Following up with the lender regularly demonstrates your commitment and eagerness to secure funding. Be prepared to provide any clarifications or address any concerns they raise during the evaluation process.

> **TOP TIP**
>
> To increase your chances of obtaining favourable loan terms, consider submitting your application to multiple lenders simultaneously. This allows you to compare offers and negotiate terms that best suit your business's needs. However, be cautious not to submit too many applications, as this may negatively impact your credit score and appear desperate to potential lenders.

OK, so you know roughly what you need to do to move forward with your plans for world domination in business, and the next step is to take action.

Summary

- When applying for a loan, seek professional guidance if needed and

THE LOAN PROCESS: NAVIGATING THE FINAL STAGES

ensure that all parties involved have signed the loan documents as required.

- Research helps ensure that you target lenders who are most likely to understand and support your business's growth objectives.

- By satisfying the lender's approval conditions, you increase the likelihood of securing the loan and moving forward with your business's growth and expansion plans.

PART FOUR
GROW

We are now ready to explore the five steps to growing any business. Alongside your growth model, we will look at your personal growth, too, which should never be ignored on your journey to business success.

11
Growing Safely, And In The Right Order

When looking to borrow for growth and expansion, it is crucial to be clear about what you are trying to achieve. Clearly defined objectives serve as a compass, guiding your efforts and aligning them with your desired outcomes. In this section, we will explore the importance of setting clear objectives in the context of business lending, discuss key considerations for defining objectives, and highlight how they can drive successful business growth.

The 5 Stages of Growth Model

We use a proprietary model called 'The 5 Stages of Growth Model' shown in the diagram below. While this is Grow Capital's specific model, the principles and drivers are much the same for any business and in most industries.

We provide our clients with tools, worksheets and calculators to use in their businesses to get a visual representation of the important levers and objectives.

Stage 1: Measure

There is an old saying in business and life that goes: 'What gets measured, gets managed'. In business, there are a few key areas we need to measure closely, and these form the 'dashboard' of your business's success. The first of these areas is to have measured and metricated *goals* (Chapter 14 is dedicated to goal-setting). By having specific and measured goals for your business, you know how the business is progressing towards its targets and are aware of any changes that need to be made. We can then reverse engineer a

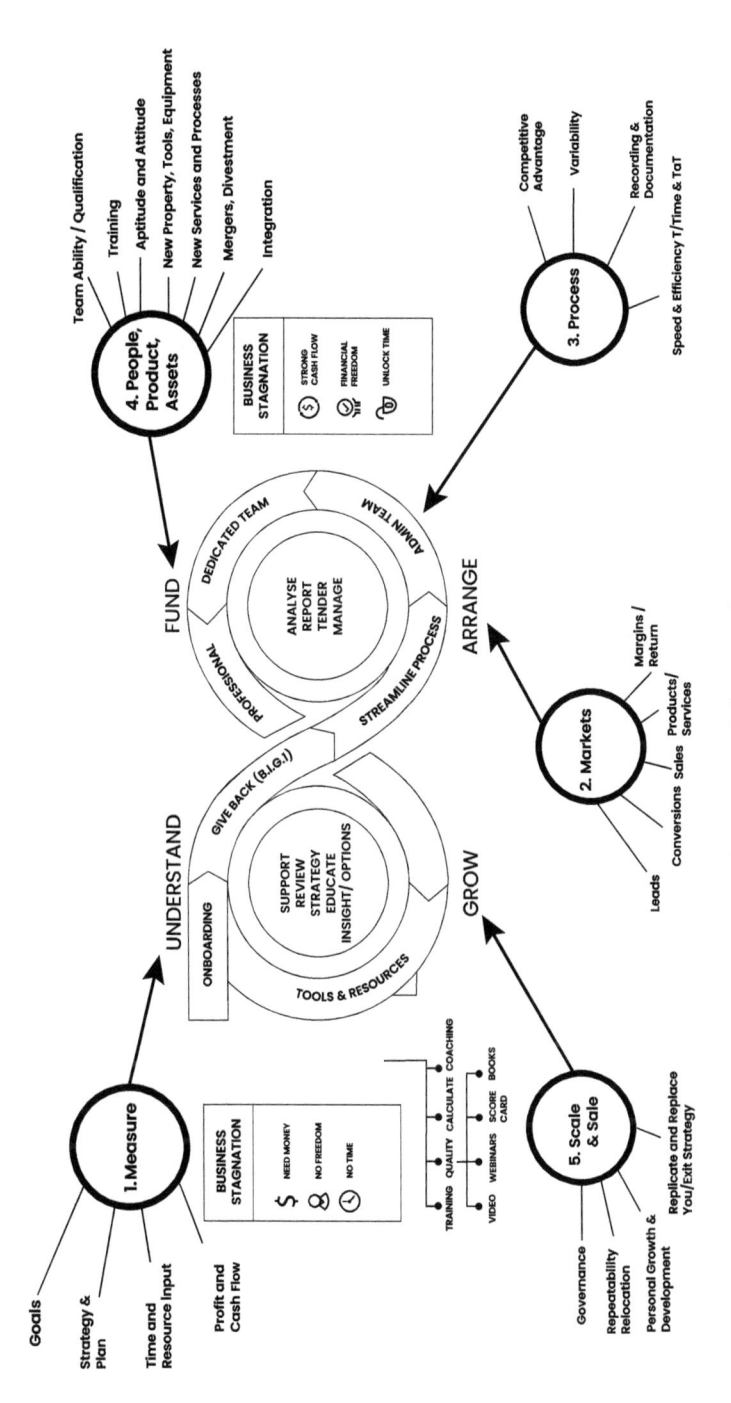

The five stages of the growth process

measured strategic plan in order for the business to hit the business goals.

In order to manage *business profit and loss* you need to carefully monitor the margins of our products and/or services, the total business income, and all of the costs associated with earning the income in each period.

EXAMPLE

You want to sell a business in three years' time for $1m and you know that the business sale multiple is the lower of:

- 3.5 times the year-three business profit
- $2,000 per onboarded business client

That means, by year three, the business needs to have both:

- At least 500 clients (500 x 2000 = $1m)
- A net profit of almost $300,000 ($300,000 x 3.5 = $1,050,000)

You now have a three year measured goal for your business forecasting. You also have something solid to work towards from day one, and, before you get too far into the business, you can test that goal to see how realistic it is.

Stage 2: Markets

Markets really are the lifeblood of any business. There is another saying that goes, 'Cash flow solves a lot of problems in business'.

Our 'contestable market' is the name for the customers or clients that could buy our product or service. To differentiate your business from competitors in a market, you need to have a 'value proposition' or 'unique selling proposition' – something that will make a customer buy from us over our competitors, assuming all other things are equal... Something that makes us stand out from our competitors. This could be a patented product, it could be an unbelievably friendly and professional service, or it could be a myriad of other things.

You can have the best product or service in the world, but if your contestable market is too small, there won't be enough people who want or need to buy from you, and you will struggle to grow your business – in fact, you will more than likely stop trading at some point in the future.

Industry benchmarking and research reports can be bought from research houses (such as

FUNDING BUSINESS GROWTH

IBIS World and Dunn and Bradstreet) and are great ways to investigate the depth of your contestable market. Once you know there is a deep enough demand for your business, the next step is to understand what it costs to acquire a client and how much a client is worth to the business. There are a few important areas you need to measure here:

- How many of your leads are generated from each marketing initiative.
- The total cost of the marketing initiative needed in order to generate the leads.
- How many leads a salesperson in the company needs to talk to in order to get a sale.
- The staff and systems costs required to get a sale.

EXAMPLE

In a basic example of the above, let's say you are running a digital advertisement for a business. Here's how it breaks down:

- The ad runs for a week and costs: $1000
- The ad generates 200 leads: $5 per lead

GROWING SAFELY, AND IN THE RIGHT ORDER

- The average salesperson takes a month to call the leads
- The salesperson's wages, time and systems costs: $5000
- The salesperson converts 10% of the 200 leads into clients, so you have twenty new clients
- Cost per client in this example: ($1000+$5000 / 20) = $300

How do you know if the business is viable? You need to understand the lifetime value of the clients (and in the above instance, it needs to be greater than $300).

A basic formula for lifetime client value (LTV) is:

> Profit generated by the customer each year
> ×
> Number of years (on average) that they are a customer
> ×
> Number of times they buy in the time they are a customer
> −
> Cost to acquire the customer

The customer lifetime value of this customer would therefore be calculated as:

$500 × 2.5 × 1 − $300 = $950 LTV

Stage 3: Process

Once you know the business is viable and potentially profitable, it is important to have clearly defined processes and systems in place. We don't earn money until a client gets through a sales/service process successfully.

To set up a great process, you need to ask target clients what they need, how they would want that delivered to them in a 'perfect package', how soon they need it, and what they are reasonably able and willing to pay for it. You can then work backwards to provide the client with what they want in the most 'frictionless' way possible, in the fastest timeframe, while maintaining quality.

Important areas to measure in systems and processes are touch time (how many steps and people are involved), turnaround time (for each step, each person involved, and for the entire process), variability (does the process change too much?) and wastage (are there unnecessary steps/people or items involved?).

By recording the steps of the delivery process for a successful sale/service, you create a template that can be replicated, tested and refined from one client to dozens or even thousands.

If you have customers that love your unique selling proposition and also get a great experience through a refined and slick process they love, you can quickly build a big following of raving fans and a big business as a result.

Stage 4: People, product, assets

Once your clients are buying from you and you start giving them what you think they want, you will quickly find gaps in your products and services. The feedback loop generally continues and opportunities will present themselves to build out new areas of the business. The types of gaps that present themselves could be numerous, including timing, communication, staffing skills or missing parts of a product.

Opportunities might include such things as clients asking for corresponding or adjoining products or services – the products and services that they historically buy elsewhere, or perhaps new products or services that don't yet exist.

EXAMPLE

You own a successful real estate agency and your clients are buying properties. In order to buy properties, the majority of buyers need finance approval.

You have heard numerous clients mention that they had trouble getting finance approval, so you introduce a new finance arm of your business to streamline that process.

You also know that half of your clients are buying properties to live in. When they buy the property, they will need removalists and cleaners. You might therefore consider venturing into those areas, too.

Having clear process maps in your business is critical not only for management, but for training and asset and resource allocation. It's imperative that the processes and procedures also include the specific team members (current and proposed) who are responsible and accountable for the various steps, as well as the specific business assets required.

EXAMPLE

If part of your process is to collect a completed item from the end of the production line, box it and deliver it to the customer, you need the following details:

- Where should it be picked up? (Provide a specific location in the factory.)
- Who picks it up?
- What skills do they need to have?
- What are they picking up specifically? (Provide a checklist of items.)
- How do they transport it? (Which business vehicle do they use?)
- How long should this take them?
- Who do they call if they have any problems or questions?
- How do they hand it over to complete their task?

Stage 5: Scale and sale

Scale

Now you have a profitable, growing and systemised business that is duplicatable, you are potentially in the scaling phase. Two important questions to ask yourself to clarify this point are:

1. Can the business survive without your involvement?
2. Can the business grow and scale without your day-to-day involvement?

If the answer to these questions is no, you still have systems, staff and processes to put in place. For a business to scale effectively, 'repeatability' in your business is essential, and as a business owner, you can only be in so many places at once.

If you can take yourself out of the day-to-day running of the business, not only do you have more time to work 'on' the business itself (as opposed to 'in it'), but there is much less limitation on your ability to scale the business fast.

If the answer to those questions is yes, a common 'next step' is to look at expanding, and acquiring more business in different geographical locations – either locally or even in different countries. This type of scaling and growth generally presents some different pressures and challenges.

A multisite, larger business would generally have an increased requirement for leadership and management. This not only adds a layer of complexity, but it also adds a layer of cost. Good managers and leaders are generally fairly expensive and need to be factored into financial growth plans.

Business reporting and corporate governance generally needs to be quite detailed for larger businesses as there are different profit and cost centres, legal jurisdictions, tax environments etc. This may mean better IT systems and finance systems are required in order to be effective. You might need to establish a company board or advisory board in one or more of the locations, or in your head office.

Given the business is now getting larger, you might also need to consider changing the way parts of the business are run – are there aspects of the business that should be outsourced or insourced to make the growth faster, easier and more economical?

EXAMPLE

An owner of a successful single site F&B (food and beverage) operation, such as a licensed restaurant, might have an in-house kitchen for that site. If the restaurant owner wants to scale and open three more sites in the local area, they would generally move to a centralised commercial kitchen that supplies all four sites daily.

The benefits of this central-kitchen model are:

- The costs of the goods can be managed down due to high volumes
- Staff are centralised and not duplicated in kitchens
- Larger, more efficient machinery (such as commercial ovens and production lines) can be used
- The repeatability and quality control are managed effectively, covering all sites

The disadvantages of a central kitchen are that:

- If the kitchen shuts down, it would affect all four sites
- If there were contaminants in the food, it could spread to all four sites

Other ways to scale a business might include merging with other business(es) and or acquiring other business(es) (called mergers and acquisitions or 'M&A'). Often, M&A strategies aim to scale businesses fast (as opposed to waiting for organic growth) as the target businesses are generally already operating and don't require time to 'trade up'. That said, it is worthwhile looking closely at the risks associated with integrating systems and people from different businesses – this can cause significant delays and cost overruns to a growth strategy.

Sale

Now you have a large, growing business that doesn't need you in it, you have a really big question to answer – do you keep the business and grow it, or do you prepare it for sale?

So why on Earth would anyone want to sell a profitable growing business? There are several reasons:

- Running larger businesses with multimillion-dollar turnovers, a larger staff and high stress levels requires a different skillset to running a small business with a few staff.

- Business owners have often worked hard for many years and want a break to do something different for a while.

- Personal challenges such as illness, partnership breakdown and divorce, and other changes in life circumstances.

- The business owners might want the financial liquidity to unlock some personal financial opportunities.

On the flipside, why would someone want to buy/acquire multiple businesses? Again, there are many reasons:

- **Input cost savings:** Bigger companies have larger buying/bargaining power with suppliers for inputs. Bigger businesses generally get cheaper goods.

- **Optimised workforce:** Acquiring multiple businesses allows for better staff distribution and technology integration, potentially reducing overall staffing needs across the group.

- **Access to finance and funding:** The larger the business, the more financing options are available and the more customisation this allows. For example, a larger company can not only borrow at lower rates, they can also list on a stock exchange to raise larger sums of money.

- **Larger sale prices:** Small to medium businesses are generally seen as 'riskier' and 'untested' in comparison to big business (for all of the reasons we have talked about above). A business turning over $1m might sell for between two and three-and-a-half times its net profit. The same business with a net profit of, say, $10m, might get a multiple of eight to ten times its profit via a trade sale, and a business with $100m profit might get twelve to fifteen times its profit via a public listing.

If you decide to put a business up for sale, before going too far down the track you would want to talk with an exit advisory specialist in the specific industry, as well as legal, tax and financial advisors to make sure the process is correct, and your expectations around sale cost, sale price range, terms and timing are acceptable.

Key principles for growth planning

Growth isn't just about getting bigger; it's about doing it in the right way and in the right order. Scale too fast without a solid foundation, and you could end up with cash flow problems, operational bottlenecks and a whole lot of stress. But when you plan properly, growth becomes sustainable and profitable. Let's look at three key principles:

1. **Aligning financing needs:** Growth requires the right funding at the right time. If lenders and investors understand your growth plan, they can offer financing that supports your business instead of slowing it down.

2. **Strategic planning:** 'We'll figure it out as we go' is not a strategy. Savvy business owners map out what they need, when they need it and how they'll deliver it.

3. **Communication and collaboration:** Scaling a business is a team effort. The

clearer your vision, the easier it is to get buy-in from lenders, investors and your team, so everyone is moving in the same direction.

Planning is just one part of the equation. To grow safely, you also need to define exactly what you're aiming for. That's where your growth objectives come in.

Key considerations for defining growth objectives

While keeping these principles in mind, knowing your objectives for growth is just as crucial. Without clear objectives, even the best strategy can fall apart. Your growth objectives act as the blueprint that guides your decisions and helps you measure success. Here's what to focus on:

- **Quantifiable growth targets:** Be specific. Are you aiming to increase revenue by 20%? Expand into new markets? Launch a new product? Setting clear, measurable targets ensures you know what success looks like and keeps you accountable.

- **Financial performance metrics:** Growth isn't just about more revenue; it's about profitability and stability. Identify key metrics like gross margin, ROI and cash flow targets to ensure your expansion is financially viable. Lenders and investors look at these numbers to assess your growth potential and risk level.

- **Market expansion and competitive advantage:** Growing safely means knowing where and how you'll compete. Are you targeting new customer segments? Entering untapped markets? Strengthening your brand positioning? Defining these objectives demonstrates that you're thinking long-term and strategically.

- **Operational efficiency and scalability:** Growth is only sustainable if your systems and processes can handle it. Set objectives around improving efficiency, optimising resources and implementing scalable systems – things that lenders and investors love to see because they signal long-term success.

- **Risk management:** Every business faces risks, but the best ones plan for them.

Identify potential risks early and outline how you'll mitigate them. Lenders value businesses that take a proactive approach to risk management because it signals stability and reliability.

- **Bringing it all together:** Smart growth isn't accidental, it's intentional. By focusing on the right principles and setting clear, measurable objectives, you give your business the best chance to scale sustainably, profitably and with minimal risk.

Plan well. Grow safely. Stay in control.

Driving successful business growth

You have a business. You want it to be successful. You want it to grow. To achieve those goals, keep in mind the following:

- **Have actionable plans:** Translate your objectives into actionable plans with clear timelines, milestones and responsibilities. Break down larger objectives into smaller, achievable tasks that can be executed incrementally.

- **Regularly monitor and evaluate your progress:** Continuously monitor progress towards your objectives and regularly assess whether adjustments are needed. This allows you to stay on track and make informed decisions based on real-time data and market dynamics.

- **Stay adaptable and agile:** Maintain flexibility and adaptability in response to changing market conditions or unforeseen challenges. Review your objectives periodically and modify them if necessary to ensure they remain relevant and aligned with your business's evolving needs.

Summary

- Having clear objectives is essential when seeking business lending for growth. Aligning financing needs and strategic planning, and fostering effective communication, can increase your chances of securing far more appropriate funding and drive successful business growth.

GROWING SAFELY, AND IN THE RIGHT ORDER

- Consider manageable and identifiable growth targets, financial performance metrics, market expansion strategies, operational efficiency, scalability plans and risk management.

- If you can translate these objectives into actionable plans and continuously monitor your progress, you can effectively navigate the lending process and achieve sustainable business growth.

12
Putting Money To Work

Traditionally, an asset is something of value that is owned by a business and that sits in the asset column of the balance sheet. A traditional asset has value, yet it doesn't always have the capacity to generate or support revenue.

We take a different approach to this, defining an ASSET as anything that generates, or supports the generation of, revenue in a business.

EXAMPLE

A construction company buys a famous piece of artwork for $10,000 to hang on the wall of their boardroom. This is an asset and can be sold, potentially for a profit.

This artwork would probably not be classed as an ASSET, as it is unlikely to directly generate or support the generation of revenue.

An art gallery buys the same famous piece of artwork for $10,000 to hang on the wall of their boardroom. This artwork consistently promotes the intangible process of selling to customers while they are in the boardroom, therefore can be assigned as an ASSET as it helps to generate revenue.

ASSETS can differ from sector to sector, as the example above shows. However, here are some generic examples that would fit into most businesses:

- Sales staff meeting KPIs
- Unique marketing collateral
- A system or process
- A popular website landing page
- A large Instagram or Twitter following
- A domain name
- Intellectual property (IP)

When you understand what an ASSET is, you will start to understand the importance of building ASSETS for any entrepreneur looking to scale their business.

> **TOP TIP**
>
> Build or buy assets that generate revenue when you are not there.
>
> Whether you are building up a team or buying an item, always keep this sage advice in mind as it will serve you well as your business grows.

Be aware of opportunities

Most business owners stick to their primary line of business when expanding or scaling their business. The reason for this is that their energy remains focused on the thing they know best and the thing that their business is set up to do. However, the history books are littered with examples of leaders who have tried to run with a new shiny opportunity to the detriment of their healthy and growing business.

FUNDING BUSINESS GROWTH

So, what do you do if you uncover an amazing opportunity right when you are in the middle of growing your business?

Many entrepreneurs have shown that, while it is difficult, it is not impossible to take on a side project while maintaining the core business. Here are some hard-hitting discussion points to hopefully provide you with enough gold to allow you to make the right call if you uncover an opportunity:

- **Should you hand over executive control?**
    - Do you need to make all the decisions?
    - Could someone do a better job than you?
    - Would you be more valuable in an advisory role?

- **Should you gift ownership of the business?**
    - Do you really need to own 100% of the business?
    - How could receiving a percentage of your profit affect the performance or mindset of a star employee?
    - 50% of a growing business is better than 100% of a dead business.

- **Should you automate everything?**
  - Can you hire someone to take on 90% of the work you do?
  - Can you build systems to automate the business?
  - Can you build processes that remove you from the workflow?
  - Will automation really release you to take on a new opportunity?

> **TOP TIP**
>
> A company is only as good as its people, so hire people that will make the company thrive, and give back to them what they put in.

OK, now that you have released your precious time, you can take on new opportunities like a true entrepreneur.

Start in the same way that you did with your first business – build a plan:

- Lay the plan out on paper or on a whiteboard.
- Workshop the idea with trusted sources to validate it.

- Build a list of to-do items in order of priority.
- Act on step one immediately.

As Sir Richard Branson says: 'Opportunities are like buses – there's always another one coming!'[5]

90-day strategic review

When was the last time that you reviewed your business's backend?

If there is one thing that most business owners neglect, it is the ongoing review of all the different aspects of their business, because the list is long, and it takes energy away from generating revenue.

Here is a quick (yet far from exhaustive) checklist of some items that we recommend you review in the next three months:

---

[5] R Branson, 'How do you train your brain to think inventively?' [LinkedIn post] (September 2024), www.linkedin.com/posts/rbranson_innovation-creativity-ideas-activity-7235219235088523264-cBht, accessed 8 May 2025

- Strategic plan
- Marketing
- Tax and accounting
- Return on investment(s) (ROI)
- Staff
- Terms of trade
- Real estate
- Insurance policies
- Finance facilities
- Technology
- Legal
- Lessons learned

How prepared will you be for the next twelve months if you spend time working through each part of your business as it relates to the list above? You will have many more items that pertain to your business, so list them down as you remember them and schedule an annual meeting.

Some of the items above will be managed externally by your panel of advisors. These advisory roles play an important role in the growth and success of your business. It is important that you select the right advisor for you and your business. Some advisors attempt to create a one-stop shop for all business owners, and while this may suit your business, we recommend selecting one based on the individual's skills and track record.

An SME's advisory panel should consist of:

- An accountant – for tax, accounting and structuring
- A solicitor – for legal advice, contracts and disputes
- A finance broker – for debt management and asset purchases
- A business advisor – for coaching, motivation, personal and business advice
- An insurance broker – for insurance policy management

It's now game on

Congratulations! Your plans have merit, the application was successful, you have an approval from your funding partner and the funds will land in your account in three days.

Now what?

With many business owners, a small nuke will go off as they realise that they now need to deliver on their promises… This is a powerful signal that means you are outside your comfort zone and ready to act. Now is the time to revert to your initial plans for the capital injection. Here are a few things to think about:

- What is the first step I need to take?
- How do I build a team fast?
- How rapidly do I scale the team?
- How long will it take to get assets and resources on the ground?
- What systems do I need to put in place to manage the growth?
- Will the current processes function effectively at scale?

The deployment of funds is a dangerous time as there is usually a large sum of money in the bank, and without careful planning, deft action

FUNDING BUSINESS GROWTH

and loads of restraint, funds can very quickly slip through the cracks before the revenue starts arriving. This is why it is so important to have a plan and stick to it. Sounds simple, doesn't it...

EXAMPLE

Jimmy's Cranes is a thriving business, supplying twenty-five-ton 'pick and carry' cranes to the booming commercial construction industry in Sydney. Jimmy has won a contract to spin up a new line of business, supplying tower cranes to his clients.

The head contractor wants five tower cranes for a new project in Parramatta, providing a fantastic opportunity for the new line of business in terms of revenue, but also being *very* visible from a marketing standpoint.

Jimmy's finance broker arranges the funding line for the purchase and delivery of the five cranes, which are on track for delivery. Jimmy also needs working capital to start hiring operators, a commissioning team, transport contractors, insurance etc... the list goes on. His finance broker arranged a business loan to provide Jimmy with the capital to get going.

Jimmy has over $1m in the bank and realises that his office is too small, and his work vehicle doesn't really represent his growing business.

He signs a lease on a large new office space and orders a fancy 4x4 with all the trimmings, including sign writing.

Everything is going well; the team is being built and it's five days from the delivery of the first crane when Jimmy realises that his account is almost empty and he needs to pay the delivery costs for the cranes. Jimmy has put the whole business operation in jeopardy.

Summary

- Just because you are working for money, doesn't mean you need to become a slave to it.

- Once you have achieved your funding goal and the money is in the bank, put the money to work for you and release yourself from the grind just enough to build and grow your empire.

- Bear in mind this simple set of guidelines to get you on the right path:
    - Deploy funds for growth strategically.
    - Build a dream team.
    - Focus on assets.
    - Identify new areas of opportunity.
    - Review your strategy and progress.

13
Personal Growth

Let's now focus on you. Along with business growth, personal growth is a goal that most entrepreneurs seek, and the key reason why we created this book. We have developed a range of thought items that are designed to get you thinking about your growth, what it looks like and how it will come to fruition.

We recommend that you take some time to go through this chapter – it is not a fast process, and it will take anywhere from a few hours to a few months to nail it down properly. Be patient, it will work.

There are a range of concepts that you need to understand when it comes to personal growth, and you need to start putting energy towards them. We will dive into each of these in the section below, including giving you some homework to do!

Vision

What is your *why*? Why are you doing what you do?

The answer to this is important, because your *why* will define the *how*. The *how* will define the *when*. The *when* will promote action.

Define your vision first – and remember that the biggest vision wins. Start to create a vision of yourself, physically, mentally, spiritually and emotionally. This new vision is likely to change as you move through the process, sometimes imperceptibly, so it is important to get your vision written down so you can review it and reflect. For example, many who embark on their first goal-setting challenge cite 'being rich or wealthy' as their driving vision, or 'being famous', and then, as time goes on, they realise that there is an emptiness inside and their goals start to shift.

> ### TASK: Create your Vision Statement
>
> A vision statement:
>
> - Ensures you stay on track
> - Helps you to push through the tough moments
> - Acts as a rock to cling to when fear sets in
> - Provides a reference point for gauging your growth
>
> Look at all the roles that you play in your life – for example, child, sibling, spouse, parent, boss, worker, volunteer, mentor, citizen, investor etc.
>
> Write these down as a list and make notes on each item, detailing what you see as a vision of yourself in each role. Start to define a vision statement, which will take some time to craft. This statement is a summary of who you want to be and what you want to achieve in life.
>
> Here's an example:
>
> Every day I work towards the values of [insert values] in all that I do. I am filled with vitality and passion when I [insert passions]. Each week I grow in the key areas of my life

> including [insert areas of focus]. I feel content and I enrich each day because I capitalise on my natural strengths of [insert strengths] by doing [insert how you apply these strengths in your work and home life]. I'm continuously developing [insert skills] for the sheer joy of doing something I love.

Drivers

What drives you or motivates you to do the things that you do? Is it money, power or prestige? Or perhaps it's happiness, freedom and well-being? You need to be clear about what gets you out of bed in the morning.

> **TASK: Identify the things that drive you**
>
> Look back at the previous task and look again at your roles. Write down which of these really drives you to do what you do.
>
> You may have only one or two primary drivers, or you may find that you have a whole range of drivers. Identifying and repairing any conflicting motivations will help to supercharge your personal growth.

PERSONAL GROWTH

Values

Label your core values. Your values govern who you are; they are the beliefs or opinions that you hold regarding specific objects, ideas or issues, and they are subjective, internal and often malleable. Get crystal clear on what values you have, as these will fuel your vision and assist with the goals.

What are values? Here are some common ones to get you thinking: honesty, loyalty, integrity, positivity, reliability, perseverance, respect, family, freedom, security, connection, creativity, humanity etc.

> **TASK: Identify your values**
>
> Pull out your roles list again and start thinking about your values. I find it useful to search for an online list of values to get some ideas. Try to get fifty on a page.
>
> Now try to boil these down to the ones that are really meaningful, and remember that they are likely to change as you go through the process of personal growth.

Goals

Goals are commonly defined as 'the object of a person's ambition or effort; an aim or desired result'. Goals give you an object to work towards, something to aim for, and if you document them, they can serve as a measuring stick to show you where you have been.

The next chapter will deep dive into how to set and review goals.

Blocks

Everybody has subconscious blocks, usually stemming from a childhood event or more recent experience – some kind of external or environmental factor, or even just a well-meaning comment from a family member or friend that gets stuck in one's subconscious mind. Examples of common blocks are guilt, shame, fear, grief and doubt. Deep-seated emotional blockages usually sit below conscious thought, so you have absolutely no idea that they're there.

Guilt and shame – two very common blocks – can even boil up into the conscious mind, and there are many things we might feel guilty or shameful about. But it's the underlying subconscious blocks that we want to be aware of.

How do you repair/remove blocks? This is a complicated task and well beyond the scope of this book. Depending on the severity of the blocks you may have, it's recommended to seek the help of a professional.

Habits

Habits are settled or regular tendencies or practices, especially ones that are hard to give up... or hard to create. Habits can be formed, and habits can be broken. This knowledge is powerful, and with it you can supercharge your personal growth.

Based on two studies from 2009 and 2021, it takes an average of sixty-six days to build/break a habit.[6,7] The range varied

---

[6] UCL News, 'How long does it take to form a habit?' (4 August 2009), www.ucl.ac.uk/news/2009/aug/how-long-does-it-take-form-habit

[7] B Singh et al, 'Time to form a habit: A systematic review and meta-analysis of health behaviour habit formation and its determinants', *Healthcare (Basel)*, 12/23 (2024), https://pmc.ncbi.nlm.nih.gov/articles/PMC11641623, accessed 8 May 2025

between eighteen and 254 days, and this variability is based on the individual, the habit, the environment etc.

So how long can you work on a goal, task or habit? We recommend thirty days for newbies, sixty days if you have already built some good habits, and ninety days if you are a legend.

> **TASK: Identify your habits**
>
> What are three habits you want to create, and three you want to break?
>
> Reflect on the list of roles you came up with earlier and pick one habit you want to break and one you want to create for each role.
>
> Examples of habits you might want to break include smoking, over-eating or drinking to excess. Habits you might want to create could include doing more exercise, taking up meditation or eating more healthily.

Verticals

The most common goal verticals are money, health and lifestyle – people generally start off wanting to be rich, slim and have a big house and car.

> **TOP TIP**
>
> Your goals will likely not all be in one area of your life, and they will shift and change as you grow.

When approaching this process, it's best to start looking at different areas of your life, like family, work, community and your environment to get you started. You can also add in money, health and lifestyle, as these are often strong drivers for some.

Congruency

Congruency is the agreement or harmony of two things. In this context, we are talking about your principles vs your actions. To ensure you have the best chance of success with your goals, you will need to aim for 100% congruency between your principles and values. What does this mean? It means do what you say or think – and think or say what you do.

For example, if you are focusing on the values of honesty and integrity to drive the direction of your goals, but in your day-to-day dealings with people you don't always act with these values in mind, then there will be a conflict – this is not congruent with the values you hold.

Fit vs healthy vs well-being

There is a general understanding in our society that someone who is physically fit is healthy, and someone who is healthy is living in a state of well-being.

While it is possible that these three things are linked, they are in fact separate, and each one should be approached individually to ensure a balanced result.

- Fitness = how you move
- Health = what you consume
- Well-being = how you think

When someone is fit, they are generally physically strong and flexible, and they recover quickly from injury. Their body is biomechanically tuned and able to withstand the stressors of exercise for longer periods of time and recover a lot faster than someone who is less fit.

When someone is healthy, they are generally consuming things that will help them to thrive, and avoiding things that can damage and age the body. This is a complex topic and well beyond the scope of this book, yet it's safe to say that healthy eating is an individual thing – you need to find out what makes your body strong and consume more of it. These things may be elusive if you are new to this practice, we will help to guide you.

> **TOP TIP**
>
> When someone is said to be in a state of well-being, their mindset is positive and they are happy and content most of the time. Achieving this isn't just about thinking happy thoughts, it's a long-term practice of doing the things that nourish your soul and make you happy.

Self-mastery

After goals are set, you need to have a clear strategy for bringing them to fruition. There is no free ride here, and the more energy you put into this, the greater the rewards you will reap from the process.

We recommend using an accountability tool to manage your daily goal and mastery process.

Five steps to self-mastery

1. Run through the first section of this chapter on understanding personal growth. This will help you to document all the bits and pieces you will need.

2. Perform the goal-setting section of the chapter. This is where you get crystal clear on what you want to get done, and how long you will be getting it done for.

3. Map out your goals on a spreadsheet or goal-tracker app, in any order that suits you. List each of your daily goals, each in its own column, and give each day a row, where you rank your daily level of achievement for each goal (from zero to ten). At the end of each day, complete the row. This kind of detail is important when it comes to reflection and review, as you can see how you are tracking. We have put an example layout for you.

Example goal tracker

Date	Goal 1: Exercise	Goal 2: Reading	Goal 3: Journaling	Goal 4: Meditating
Day 1	2	6	7	9
Day 2	7	3	2	2
Day 3	6	5	6	8
Day 4	9	6	2	8
Day 5	3	7	8	1

4. Start. Today… Yes, today! Procrastination is the single deadliest killer of dreams. You don't have to be perfect – even if you only do one goal today, you have taken the first step.

5. Do the work. Rinse and repeat until complete. You may want to consider adding in a few extra items on top of your goals, particularly if your goals are all related to your finances and your work.

Non-negotiables

Here are some things that I consider to be the non-negotiables in my daily routine/self-mastery:

- Meditate every day.
- Practise daily visualisation.
- Exercise daily, whether walking, running, riding, swimming, or doing yoga or Pilates.
- Eat clean and nutritional food.
- Stay hydrated.
- Do something good every day, like starting a conversation with a stranger or doing a random act of kindness.
- Learn something every day. Read ten pages of a book – ideally a nonfiction book (eg a biography of a successful person or something motivational), or research a new subject or topic you don't know much about for fifteen minutes.

Finally...

Reviewing your goals and how often you review them (whether that's three, six or twelve months) are important. Reaching goals will create new paths, and this will require constant monitoring and reviewing of your habits, values, diet, exercise programme, principles etc. Here are some things to bear in mind:

- Resetting goals can be a fun and exciting experience.
- It's important to document the process so you can reflect and review it in the future.
- The largest vision wins – aim big!
- Most people overestimate what they can do in a day, and underestimate what is possible in a year.
- Big, lofty goals will likely take you further ahead than small, conservative goals.
- Reflect on your progress.
- Look back at the process to see where you have come from and what you have achieved.
- Celebrate your achievements.

Give yourself a pat on the back, go out for a night out, take a holiday or buy yourself something nice to celebrate the amazing work you have done. Celebrating your achievements has a subconscious impact on you, reinforcing that the changes are positive and making it a little easier to harden down a habit on the next cycle.

Keep a 'done list' of all the goals you've achieved – documenting the completion process is a powerful tool. It is critical, in fact, to allowing you to reflect on your achievements.

Summary

- Your vision is who you want to become, what you want to be doing, where you want to live, who you want to spend your time with, who you want to help… and the list goes on.

- Everyone has their own motivation; there is no right or wrong.

- Consistent daily action is the only way to progress towards your goals.

14
Goal-Setting 101

This is where the rubber meets the road... and you start setting some goals!

Over the last ten years, working closely with business owners and entrepreneurs on their growth and success, we started to see some clear patterns emerge that really made a mark. It became clear to us that those who set goals, reviewed them consistently and reframed them on a regular basis, were more likely not just to hit those targets, but were also successful in all areas of their business and personal life.

Out of this, we developed a goal-setting protocol which has morphed into an effective goals programme that is constantly being tested, and that consistently delivers results for our business owners and entrepreneurs, and now it is available to you!

Follow it, persevere through your doubts, and you are guaranteed to see change.

Define your goals

The first challenge you'll face in this goal-setting process is identifying exactly what your goals are. This will involve a brainstorming process which could take five minutes, five days or five weeks, depending on who you are.

The seven-step process that we use for all our goal-setting is set out below. Follow the bouncing ball, have fun along the way, and push through to the end as it will all be worth it:

1. Brainstorm your SMART goals
2. Boil it down to the top ten goals
3. Frame each goal

4. Set timeframes

5. Set accountability

6. Do the work

7. Reflect, review, reset, restart

Brainstorm your SMART goals

SMART is an acronym used globally for setting any type of goal. To make sure your goals are impactful and achievable, each of them should be:

- **Specific:** Who will do what, when, where, why? Act like a laser beam – be focused and accurate.

- **Measurable:** Ensure that you can easily measure your progress.

- **Attainable:** Set something that is challenging yet possible. As you grow, so will your goals.

- **Relevant:** How does this goal fit into your grand plan?

- **Time-based:** Lay down a deadline.

To brainstorm your SMART goals, choose three goals for each of the life areas that follow. Take your time and really think about what you want and come up with:

- One goal for now (to be achieved within the next year)
- One goal for later (to be achieved in the next two to five years)
- One big crazy goal (remember, the biggest vision wins)

Here are some examples for each life area to help stimulate the idea factory:

- Family:
    - Spend fifteen minutes each day with my children/spouse.
    - Visit my father/mother once a week.
    - Plan an overseas family holiday every six months.

- Financial:
    - Save $1000 per month for holidays.
    - Buy an investment property in three months.
    - Take a course on how to trade stocks and currencies next week.

- Physical:
  - Exercise for thirty minutes, three times a week.
  - Join a weekly yoga class.
  - Sign up for the next local marathon.

- Health:
  - Follow a healthy eating plan for thirty days.
  - Quit alcohol and cigarettes for ninety days.
  - Run a full health audit with my healthcare provider.

- Giving:
  - Give to a charity once a month.
  - Donate one hour a month to my community.
  - Sponsor a child.

- Artistic:
  - Enrol in a painting class in three weeks.
  - Write a book.

- Mindset:
  - Meditate for fifteen minutes each morning for ninety days.

- Visualise my top goal for five minutes each night for thirty days.
- Write down three things I am grateful for each morning for thirty days.

- Career:
  - Ask for a pay rise/promotion next week.
  - Have a thirty-minute brainstorming session about potential side-hustles.
  - Start a business by registering it online.

Boil it down to the top ten goals

Now you need to boil your list of goals down to your top ten. This is quite a challenging task, but we're going to help you. We have a process for this which is highly effective. Really put some time into this to decide whether you want to reach each goal now or in the future.

You should now have roughly twenty-five to thirty goals written down. So first, put them into a list – a spreadsheet is great for this. Then, take the first goal and reference it against each of the remaining goals. The aim here is to establish the importance or priority of each goal for you, personally. Give each goal one point for every goal on the list that is a lower priority and note the final score for that goal. As you move down the list you are only making comparisons with the remaining goals, not the goals that already have a score.

Once this is complete, you will have a list of goals with scores. Now take the top ten and these will be your first goals list.

Ideally, the ten goals you have now identified will be spread across the different life categories, but it is OK if you have many from a single category – it really doesn't matter, what matters is that you have ten goals that are your clear priority.

Frame each goal

To a newcomer, this section may seem frivolous or silly, yet how you label and view your goals is one of the most important parts of this whole process.

> **TOP TIP**
>
> The human mind tends to latch onto the words in any statement that are repeatedly thought or spoken, it's how we are wired.

The trick here is to frame each goal statement in terms of what you want, rather than what you don't want. This programmes your subconscious and will have a dramatic impact on the speed and direction of your goal-setting process. It is also the primary reason that so many who try setting goals give up as it simply doesn't work.

Here is an example that shows the evolution of a common goal from a negative statement into a positive one, and then from a vague statement into a SMART goal.

The initial goal: *I want to stop eating junk food.*

Let's start by reframing that in the positive: *I want to start eating healthy food.*

Great, that's a start. Now let's make our goal SMART. The goal is already relevant, being about healthy food, so we've got one of the SMART criteria ticked off.

So first, let's be more specific: *I will eat mainly whole organic food.* By adding the word 'mainly' in here, we've also hit another SMART requirement by making it more attainable.

Now let's add a timeframe, which will also make the goal measurable: *Over the next thirty days, I will eat mainly whole organic food.* That's the final two SMART elements covered.

Can you see how this statement has been manipulated to be specific (whole organic food), measurable (thirty days), attainable (mainly), relevant (food), time-based (thirty days)?

The revamped goal above is a lot more likely to have a lasting result for you.

Set timeframes

Having a timeframe wrapped around a goal, as we have just seen, is part of the SMART framework, and you should try to put a timeframe on every goal you set to give you the best chance at achieving it.

It's often said that it takes roughly twenty-eight days of consistent daily effort to create or break a habit. However, the time required can vary depending on the individual and the habit being formed or changed – some habits may take hold sooner, while others require a longer period of consistent effort.

If you apply the same principle to sixty or ninety days, then you will be building habits that will likely last the rest of your lifetime, or more importantly, removing those habits that have sabotaged your goals and dreams in the past.

Here are some examples of different goals and the timeframes we recommend you try to build or break a habit. The longer the time between each iteration of the task, the longer you will need to go to build or break the habit:

- Daily tasks: Around twenty-eight days to build initial consistency
- Tasks that you do three times a week: Sixty to ninety days to solidify the habit
- Weekly tasks: Three to six months for the behaviour to become ingrained

Set accountability

Let's say you are on day twenty-three of your sixty-day exercise routine. It has been going well until now, but today you woke up feeling flat, tired and over it. You had a bad day at work and an argument with your partner and you are ready to just throw in the towel. Who do you have keeping you accountable for completing this?

Most people lack the ability to keep themselves motivated when things get tough. There are options here, for example:

- An accountability partner – like a trainer, a friend or just someone who will call you out and motivate you to keep going
- Software/APP – a program that counts your days and kicks your ass when you fail

Taking responsibility is important if you want to give yourself the best chance at success.

Do the work

Set up a daily practice with a checklist to follow, making it as simple as possible. Reinforce your goals by running through the list daily, the gold standard is twice a day, once upon waking, and again before going to sleep.

To do this, prepare by having a whiteboard or notepad on hand. Choose a time of the day when you are calm and free of the millions of thoughts running through your mind. Try to avoid bright screens, lights, stimulants or loud music before this practice. Next, write down your top ten goals in a list. This is a daily repetitive task.

As you write each one down, really try and visualise yourself already at this goal.

> **TOP TIP**
>
> Write down your goals before a ten-minute meditation. This will help to reinforce these goals in your subconscious mind, which will help you greatly.

Reflect, review, reset, restart

OK, so you have spent the last thirty days booze-free – you're at the end of the streak and feeling great… So, what's next?

Journal your situation, how you are feeling, what you have achieved, what you have learned and how far forward you have come. Reflect on these positive writings. Gratitude is incredibly powerful at this moment, as it will reinforce what you have programmed into your skull.

What's gratitude? It's simple… here is an example: *I feel grateful that I have the mental strength and perseverance to go thirty days without alcohol.*

Write down a gratitude statement for each goal, whether you have been successful or not. Here is an example of a goal that was not achieved in the timeframe: *Although I did not last the full thirty days without alcohol, I am grateful for the health boost that I have achieved on the days I did abstain.*

Review each goal one by one, looking at it with a view to either recycling it for the next round or dropping it. You may be surprised after a few rounds of goal-setting which goals you decide to throw away and which you keep.

Reset your goals by running back through the process again from the beginning. It gets a lot easier with experience and your goals will start to be more focused and strategic.

Restart the next round as soon as you can – don't delay and dwell too long. In our observations and experience, a long delay between goal resets can create large setbacks.

Summary

- Growth can represent countless different objectives and is likely different for everyone.

- Crafting each goal to be framed in the positive will set you up for success.

- The longer you stick to something, the harder the process will be… but the deeper it will embed/break the habit.

Conclusion

Congratulations on getting this far. We know some content can be 'as dry as toast'. But we hope you agree it's been worth it.

The best thing is, getting great outcomes and financing for your business and other businesses is a framework that's now available to you. There's a reminder of the framework below.

Now that you have absorbed this knowledge, all you have to do is complete and repeat the formula whenever you need it. But before you do, let's go over a few key elements of our message. Did you realise the importance and relevance of the number five in this book? Well, here's a recap.

BUSINESS STAGNATION

- 💲 STRONG CASH FLOW
- 🚫 FINANCIAL FREEDOM
- ⏱ UNLOCK TIME

FUND

- DEDICATED TEAM
- ADMIN TEAM
- PROFESSIONAL
- STREAMLINE PROCESS

Core: ANALYSE / REPORT / TENDER / MANAGE

ARRANGE

UNDERSTAND

- GIVE BACK (B.I.G.1)
- ONBOARDING

Core: SUPPORT / REVIEW / STRATEGY / EDUCATE / INSIGHT / OPTIONS

GROW

TOOLS & RESOURCES

- TRAINING — VIDEO
- QUALITY — WEBINARS
- CALCULATE — SCORE CARD
- COACHING — BOOKS

BUSINESS STAGNATION

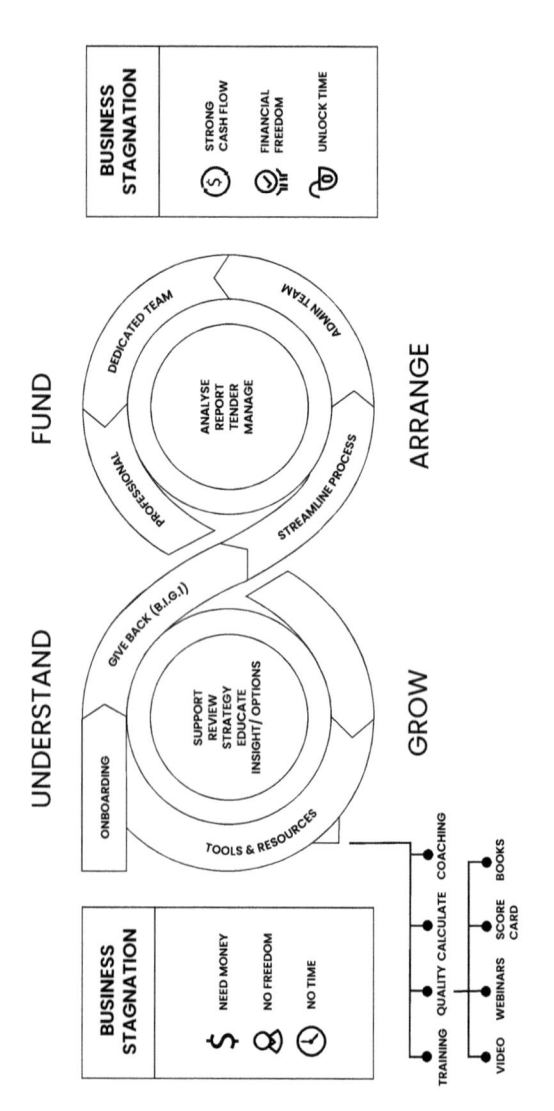

- 💲 NEED MONEY
- 🚫 NO FREEDOM
- ⏱ NO TIME

Understand, Arrange, Fund, Grow

First of all, in Chapter 3 we went into the 5Cs Credit Model in detail, but we believe they are worth a quick reminder here:

The 5Cs Credit Model:

- **Collateral:** What is securing the loan?
- **Capacity:** How will the loan be repaid?
- **Character:** What is the borrower's credit history and experience?
- **Capital:** How much is required up front?
- **Conditions:** What are the loan terms?

The tips and advice in this book have been designed with you in mind. They have worked for numerous clients. They will work for you, too.

Fast forward to Chapter 11, which included our 5 Stages of Growth Model, giving you tips on how to navigate each of the following key phases to maximise your, and your business's potential:

- Existence
- Survival

- Success
- Scale
- Maturity

Chapter 13's five steps to self-mastery (and we make no apologies for banging on about this) stressed the importance of a holistic approach that will ensure your work-life balance is healthy and that benefits everyone in your business as well as your family.

Finally, we want you to ensure that all your goals align with the five-letter acronym SMART:

- Specific
- Measurable
- Attainable
- Relevant
- Time-based

We can help you grow

By buying and reading *Funding Business Growth*, you have already invested time and money in your future. In exploring the

CONCLUSION

numerous funding options available, we hope you now feel you have the right degree of knowledge to make an informed choice that is right for your business.

Remember, your business starts and ends with you. Your business is in your hands. How that business develops and grows, and how you manage that growth, is down to you.

Through the four parts of this book (Understand, Arrange, Fund, Grow) and over the course of fifteen chapters, we have given you a template to build your business, applying our guidelines across the board. We recognise that there is a lot of content here and you probably have a few questions. If so, we'd love to hear from you. Please feel free to drop us a line and we will get back to you as fast as we can. Similarly, if you would like access to some measurement and management tools for your business or your client's business, do contact our team at fundingbusinessgrowth.com.au and we will get you access straight away.

Until then, take care and grow!

Acknowledgements

Gus Gilkeson

This book would not exist without the extraordinary people who have supported us throughout this journey.

First, to my co-author, Nick, thanks for being a great mate for the last thirty years and for co-piloting our business and journey. Life is about experiences, and this has been a rewarding and fun experience with you.

My deepest gratitude especially to my wife Georgia and girls, Mae and Lola, who endured countless late nights and working weekends while providing unwavering encouragement. Your belief in me sustained this project through its darkest moments. Thanks also to my family, Anne, Garry, Fi, Duge and Skye, who have all helped me personally and with the business in various formats over the years.

To all of my mentors, who saw potential in our ideas long before I fully believed in them myself: your guidance transformed not just this book, but my entire approach to business, finance, leadership and life.

I'm indebted to the brilliant team at Rethink Press (Joe, Lucy, Sarah, Sandra, Jonathan, Jennifer, Anke and Kathy), whose incisive feedback challenged me to dig deeper and articulate concepts with greater clarity and impact.

Special thanks to the entrepreneurs and business leaders who trusted us with their financing requirements and generously shared their stories – both triumphs and failures – with remarkable candour. Your grit, vulnerability and wisdom breathe life into these pages.

Thank you to our friends and partners who have played strategic and financial roles in our business, particularly Chrissy Lewis, Annie Gilkeson, Dave Flakelar, Stephen Choy, Frank and Patricia Kwok, Andy Edwards, Emily Edwards, Ben Freischmidt and Ian Barry.

To our brilliant team, particularly Louise, who covered for me when deadlines loomed, and to our clients, and investor and lender partners whose thoughtful questions helped refine many of the concepts presented here: thank you for being part of this intellectual journey.

Finally, to the readers who pick up this book seeking new perspectives: my hope is that these ideas serve as catalysts for your own ventures and dreams. Success is rarely a solitary achievement, and this book stands as testament to the power of community, connection and collective wisdom.

Nick Wormald

This book wouldn't have come to life without the people who've stood beside me, not just in business, but in life.

To my co-author, business partner and best mate, Gus, thank you for walking this journey with me, keeping a hand on my shoulder and guiding me through life's challenges. What began as a small seedling of an idea has grown into something far bigger than either of us imagined, and your trust, perseverance and leadership have made all the difference. I've learned a lot, and I'm proud we've done this together.

To Gemma, your patience, love and belief in me, especially on the days I was running on empty, meant more than I can say. You remind me why I do this.

To Amelia and Ben, thank you for your understanding every time I was pulled away. I hope this book shows you the value of perseverance and purpose.

To Mum and Dad, Annie and James, thank you for shaping who I am, through the huge challenges we've all faced.

To Soph, thank you for your support in the early days of building this business, when it was still taking shape. That foundation mattered more than you probably realise.

ACKNOWLEDGEMENTS

To the countless friends and mentors who saw something in me before I could see it myself, you all know who you are, and I'm incredibly thankful to have you in my life.

To my team at Grow Capital, your loyalty and dedication gave me the time and headspace to write.

To our clients, thank you for trusting us with your business and your stories. So much of what's in these pages is inspired by your drive, grit and courage.

Thanks also to the team at Rethink Press for helping shape this book into something we're proud to share.

Finally, to you, the reader. Thank you for picking up the book and turning the pages. If you're here, you're likely building something that matters.

My hope is that this book gives you fresh perspective, sharper tools and a little more belief in yourself.

Stay curious, stay focused and, above all, keep going!

The Authors

Gus Gilkeson

Gus has a background in business and property finance and a passion for helping business owners achieve financial success. With over two decades of experience in the industry, he has worked with thousands of clients from all industries and understands the unique challenges faced by business owners. Through his work as a financial broker and originator, he strives to create more equitable access to finance and resources. Gus is thrilled to be a co-author of this book, and to share his perspective and expertise with business owners everywhere.

in www.linkedin.com/in/gus-gilkeson

Nick Wormald

Nick is a seasoned expert in finance with more than ten years of diverse experience in this field. He is committed to inspiring individuals to seize command of their financial status and realise their objectives. His role as a finance broker has provided him with a profound understanding of the influence this can wield on people's lives. Nick is excited to disseminate his knowledge and insights through this book, to help business owners establish the financial resources and safety they are worthy of.

in www.linkedin.com/in/nick-wormald

www.ingramcontent.com/pod-product-compliance
Ingram Content Group UK Ltd.
Pitfield, Milton Keynes, MK11 3LW, UK
UKHW022009010725
460307UK00007B/178